Higher education: who pays? who benefits? who should pay?

A Report and Recommendations by
The Carnegie Commission on Higher Education
JUNE 1973

MCGRAW-HILL BOOK COMPANY

New York   St. Louis   San Francisco   Düsseldorf
London   Sydney   Toronto   Mexico   Panama
Johannesburg   Kuala Lumpur   Montreal
New Delhi   São Paulo   Singapore

This report is issued by the Carnegie Commission
on Higher Education, with headquarters at
2150 Shattuck Avenue, Berkeley, California 94704.
The views and conclusions expressed in this report
are solely those of the members of the Carnegie Commission
on Higher Education and do not necessarily reflect the
views or opinions of the Carnegie Corporation of New York,
The Carnegie Foundation for the Advancement of Teaching,
or their trustees, officers, directors, or employees.

Library of Congress Cataloging in Publication Data

Carnegie Commission on Higher Education.
Higher education: who pays? who benefits? who should pay?
Bibliography: p.
1.   Universities and colleges–Finance.   I.   Title.
LB2342.C26   379'.1214   73-8856
ISBN 0-07-010079-9

Additional copies of this report may be ordered from McGraw-Hill
Book Company, Hightstown, New Jersey 08520.
The price is $3.95 a copy.

Equal and exact justice to all men, of whatever state or persuasion . . .

THOMAS JEFFERSON
First Inaugural Address

Contents

Foreword, vii

1 *Major Themes*, 1

2 *The Educational Accounts*, 19

Federal research and services ▪ Sale of services ▪ Related activities ▪ Student-aid income ▪ Auxiliary enterprises ▪ Glossary of terms

3 *An Aggregate View of College Financing*, 29

4 *Capital Costs*, 35

5 *Considerations of Equity*, 39

6 *The Tax Burden*, 43

7 *Forgone Income*, 49

8 *Tuition as Income to Institutions of Higher Education*, 55

9 *User Costs for Higher Education*, 61

10 *The Benefits of Higher Education*, 71

Rates of return on the investment in human capital

11 *User Benefits versus Societal Benefits*, 79

12 *The Level and Quality of Education*, 89

13 *Graduate and Advanced Professional Education*, 93

14 *Policy Considerations and Recommendations*, 99

Policy considerations ▪ Sharing the cost burden ▪ Tuition policy ▪ Basic Opportunity Grants ▪ State policies ▪ Loan policies ▪ Cost estimates

15 *Who Does What?*, 123

The federal government ▪ State governments ▪ Colleges and universities ▪ Students and parents

Appendix A: The Consolidated Institutional Income Accounts, and Alternative Ways of Viewing the Cost Burden of Higher Education, 131

Appendix B: University Research Activities, 165

Appendix C: The Family Contribution to College Costs: 1971–72 Survey of California Students, 169

Appendix D: Estimated Distribution of Tax Burden and Institutional Subsidies, by Income Group, 175

Appendix E: Projections for 1983, 179

Appendix F: State Aid for Private Colleges and Universities, 183

References, 187

Foreword

Benefits from higher education flow to all, or nearly all, persons in the United States directly or indirectly, and the costs of higher education are assessed against all, or nearly all, adults directly or indirectly. Few Americans are denied any benefits and few adults escape any costs. The benefits take many forms and are delivered in quite unequal amounts; the costs, likewise, are assessed in many ways and in quite diverse sums. This report is concerned with the very complicated and important questions of who benefits from, who pays for, and who should pay for higher education. Our Commission in earlier reports has discussed some aspects of these questions, but never before so broadly:

In *Quality and Equality* (and in its *Revision*) we urged more support from the federal government and particularly for low-income students.

In *The Capitol and the Campus* we discussed state support in general and more aid to the private sector of higher education in particular.

We seek in this report to look at the problems of costs and benefits more in their totality than we have before, and to present a more detailed analysis than we have before of the sharing of the cost burden.

In the preparation of this report we held two conferences of experts and are indebted to the participants for their advice: Howard R. Bowen, Chancellor, Claremont University Center; Mary Jean Bowman, Professor of Economics and Education, University of Chicago; George F. Break, Chairman,

Department of Economics, University of California, Berkeley; Allan Cartter, then Chancellor, New York University; W. Lee Hansen, Professor of Economics, University of Wisconsin, Madison; Seymour E. Harris, Professor Emeritus of Economics and Medical Economics, University of California, San Diego; Fritz Machlup, Professor Emeritus of Economics, Princeton University; Joseph Pechman, Director, Economics Division, The Brookings Institution; Roy Radner, Professor of Economics, University of California, Berkeley; Theodore W. Schultz, Professor of Economics, University of Chicago; and W. Allen Wallis, President, University of Rochester. Howard Bowen, W. Lee Hansen, and Robert Hartman of The Brookings Institution also commented upon a late draft of this report.

We have also drawn on several reports prepared for the Commission, including: *Recent Alumni and Higher Education*, by Joe L. Spaeth and Andrew M. Greeley (McGraw-Hill, 1970); *Credit for College*, by Robert Hartman (McGraw-Hill, 1971); *Resource Use in Higher Education*, by June O'Neill (Carnegie Commission, 1971); *A Degree and What Else?*, by Stephen B. Withey (McGraw-Hill, 1971); *Education, Income, and Human Behavior* (tentative title), edited by F. Thomas Juster (forthcoming); and *Sources of Funds to Colleges and Universities*, by June O'Neill (1973).

In particular, we express our appreciation to the members of our staff and especially to Allan M. Cartter, Margaret S. Gordon, and Ralph Purves for assistance in preparation of this report.

Eric Ashby
The Master
Clare College
Cambridge, England

Ralph M. Besse
Partner
Squire, Sanders & Dempsey,
  Counsellors at Law

Joseph P. Cosand
Professor of Education and
  Director
Center for Higher Education
University of Michigan

William Friday
President
University of North Carolina

The Honorable Patricia
  Roberts Harris
Partner
Fried, Frank, Harris, Shriver, &
  Kampelman, Attorneys

David D. Henry
President Emeritus
Distinguished Professor of
  Higher Education
University of Illinois

Theodore M. Hesburgh,
  C.S.C.
President
University of Notre Dame

*Higher education:
who pays? who benefits?
who should pay?*

1. Major Themes

1 From the point of view of individual and national welfare, higher education is one of the most important qualitative services in the United States. Quantitatively, colleges and universities account for expenditures totaling about one-fortieth of our national production of goods and services — 2.5 percent. How higher education is financed is of substantial significance to millions of individuals and to society as a whole.

2 Higher education in the United States now costs (1970–71 data) about $22 billion in *monetary outlays* for the educational and living expenses of students. Counting also the net loss of potential income to students, the *economic costs* are about $39 billion. (For a definition of terms see Section 2.)

Monetary outlays are borne about one-third by students and their parents, and about two-thirds by public sources and philanthropy.[1] In terms of economic costs, however, the figures are reversed — students and their parents bear about two-thirds of the burden and public sources and philanthropy about one-third. (See Chart 1.)

From the point of view of social justice, the distribution of economic costs is more important than the distribution of monetary outlays alone. Thus a basic question is: are economic costs assessed in some rough proportion to benefits?

An alternative method of looking at economic costs is to count only the subsistence costs of students and not the part also of forgone earnings that exceeds subsistence costs. Such an

---

[1] Inclusion of calculated capital costs with operating costs adds about 12 to 15 percent to monetary outlays, and shifts the burden somewhat more heavily toward public sources and philanthropy, which bear a heavier share of capital costs than of operating costs.

CHART 1
Costs of higher education

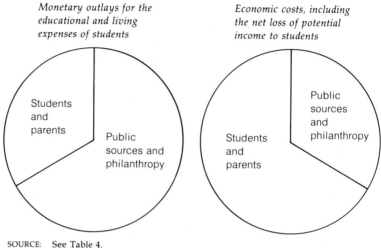

Monetary outlays for the educational and living expenses of students

Students and parents

Public sources and philanthropy

Economic costs, including the net loss of potential income to students

Public sources and philanthropy

Students and parents

SOURCE: See Table 4.

approach gives rise to a different balance between private and public total costs. We strongly favor the forgone earnings approach, however. There is a clear cost in output to the economy of college attendance as compared with the employment of students in gainful occupations. And, while it is true that the alternative to education for some students would be consumption (travel or leisure) and not work production, for most students it would be employment. And this is increasingly the situation as more students enroll from low-income families, as the average age of students rises, and as more young persons are "independent" at age 18. The economy forgoes current output and most individuals involved forgo current income.

3   Benefits take many forms. Some are individual and accrue to the direct recipients of education; among other advantages are a higher income, a more satisfying job, greater effectiveness as a consumer, greater ability in allocating time as well as money, direct enjoyment of the educational process and its related activities, and lifetime enhancement of cultural and other experiences. Some benefits are social and accrue to nonrecipients as well as to direct recipients of education; among the gains are greater economic growth based on the general advancement of knowledge and elevation of skills and on the higher proportion of the population in the labor force and the enhanced mobility

of members of the labor force; greater political effectiveness of a democratic society based on the more adequate knowledge and more active participation of citizens; greater social effectiveness of society through the resultant better understanding and mutual tolerance among individuals and groups; the more effective preservation and extension of the cultural heritage; the greater ability of individuals and groups to accept and adjust to rapid change; and the greater potential contribution of educated parents to the welfare of their children.

4   No precise—or even imprecise—methods exist to assess the individual and societal benefits as against the private and the public costs. It is our judgment, however, that the proportion of total economic costs now borne privately (about two-thirds) as against the proportion of total economic costs now borne publicly (about one-third) is generally reasonable.[2] We note that for one item—additional earned income by college graduates—about two-thirds is kept privately and about one-third is taken publicly in the form of taxes. We also note that this two-thirds to one-third distribution of total economic costs has been a relatively stable relationship for a substantial period of time (although the internal components of each share have changed—for example, the private share is now more heavily composed of forgone income and less of tuition charges). (See Chart 4.)

We see no strong reason to change this distribution in any revolutionary fashion either in the direction of full costs privately borne or full costs publicly borne, although there are forceful advocates for fundamental change in each of these directions. In the absence of stronger proof than we have seen or stronger arguments than we have heard, we accept the current distribution of burden as generally reasonable.

---

[2] Bowen and Servelle (1972, Sec. 9) have recently reached much the same conclusion: that it is reasonable to have about a two-thirds private and one-third public sharing of total economic costs.

We define *private* costs for these purposes as those borne by the family unit (parents and students), and *public* costs as those borne by governmental agencies and philanthropy. The former might alternatively be called *personal* and the latter *nonpersonal* costs. Philanthropy, of course, is a different phenomenon than direct governmental support, although about one-half of philanthropy consists of taxes forgone by public bodies. *Governmental costs* are those borne by federal, state, and local governments.

We recognize, of course, that there are some negative results of higher education—for example, the individual frustrations resulting from the current surplus of Ph.D.'s and the public unhappiness with past outbreaks of campus disruption—and we have sought to take them into account in reaching our judgment. We also recognize that, without any public subsidy, some of the social benefits of higher education would come as *side effects* of privately financed education in any case. Whether this would be entirely fair is another question. But some benefits would not come at all or at least not to the same extent, such as greater equality of opportunity through higher education and much basic research, and each of these is of great social importance.

In the absence of better knowledge about the relationships between specific subsidies and the specific social benefits that may in part or in whole be dependent upon the subsidies, it is our view that historical arrangements should not now be suddenly rearranged; that we should be cautious in what we do, and that, in any event, public opinion would need to be better prepared than it now is for any drastic changes such as full-cost pricing to the student or full-cost pricing to the public. We believe that history and myriad public and private decisions have given us, for the present time at least, a generally acceptable balance in the distribution of overall costs between the private and the public sectors as compared with the distribution of benefits.

5 We do see, nevertheless, several specific adjustments that should be made and that, if made, would yield greater justice. In their totality—and they should be viewed as a totality—these changes are both substantial and important to improved national welfare:

(1) *A temporary reduction in the comparative charge of monetary outlays to private individuals and an equivalent increase in public funding* in order to make possible the attendance of more students from low-income families dependent upon public support. We say *temporary* because the rising level of incomes will reduce over time the need for this additional public support. The current private share of monetary outlays thus might

drop somewhat and then gradually rise again. We define as *temporary* at least the next decade.

(2) *A redistribution in total governmental costs from the states and localities to the federal government.* The federal government has a larger and more expansible income than do the states and localities, and it is collected on the basis of more progressive taxes. Also the federal government has a special interest in and responsibility for equality of opportunity—this is a national promise, and the states, given their varied economic situations, cannot provide equivalent opportunities in any event. The federal government, additionally, bears responsibilities for basic research; for training of high-level and highly mobile skilled persons such as medical doctors and Ph.D.'s; for invention and innovation in the structures and processes of higher education; and for providing a nationwide student loan program. The states (and local governments) now bear the total governmental costs of higher education on a ratio of about 57.5 to 42.5 percent (see Table 1) in comparison with federal support, and we suggest that this become more nearly 50 to 50. About 20 percent of the federal 42.5 percent now takes the form of veterans' benefits; as these benefits are reduced drastically over time, the opportunity is created for the federal government to increase its funds for equality of opportunity more generally without raising the expenditures in total—about $1 billion a year is potentially available. Thus we suggest that the federal share rise to 50 percent and remain there even as veterans' benefits are reduced.

Federal interests in equality of opportunity, in basic research and in high-level professional skills, in particular, have risen over the past two decades, and the federal government, given its tax structure, also obtains most of the tax benefits from the added incomes of the more highly educated. The states now make most of the governmental investment in higher education and the federal government reaps most of the gain through tax receipts.

This is not to suggest that state effort should decline—quite the contrary; more students will be in public institutions, costs per student will rise, more state support will go to private institutions, more state tuition grants will go to students at both public and private institutions—but rather to suggest that federal effort should increase faster than state effort, particularly in the area of supporting equality of opportunity. The federal share, as we calculate it, is less than the federal government currently calculates it to be. We do not count the unsubsidized portions of federal loan programs as a federal contribution, since they are subject to repayment by the borrowers. Loans can be very helpful, but they are not gifts.

(3) *A redistribution of student subsidies in favor of those from low-income families.* Students are now subsidized indirectly through tuitions that are less than the costs of education and directly through student aid. Total subsidies may now be nearly adequate in amount, but they require some major redistribution to accomplish equity goals. Perhaps as much as two-thirds or more of all subsidies,[3] and certainly at least one-half, take the place of private expenditures, since the private expenditures would be made if the subsidies did not exist—the students would go to college in any event. These subsidies are "replacements" for private funds that would otherwise be forthcoming.

We favor a gradual redistribution of subsidies (a) by charging higher tuition to those who can afford to pay it—rising over a period of years; and (b) by providing more aid to students from lower-income families, particularly through the full funding of the Basic Opportunity Grants program provided by the Education Amendments of 1972,[4] and through liberalization, for lower-division students, of the limitation on the proportion of student costs that can be covered.

We believe that the President and the Congress made an historic step toward greater equality of opportunity through higher education in the Higher Education Act of 1972. It is of great importance that it be fully funded and that the 50-percent limitation be raised at least for lower-division students.

We believe that it is reasonable to move toward a redistribution of subsidies so that more like one-third rather than two-thirds would replace private funds. We do not believe that it is reasonable at this time to suggest that more subsidies than this be replaced by private funds that otherwise could and would be

---

[3] See Peltzman (1973).

[4] Hereafter, these amendments will be referred to as the Higher Education Act of 1972, a designation commonly used.

paid. The tradition of history is too strong in favor of broader subsidies; the politics of a democracy with a strong middle class run against it; and there are some adjustment problems, in any event, in phasing one level of subsidy into the next and then into none at all. But net subsidies (and subsidies adjusted for taxes paid) are as great for families in middle-income groups as they are for those from the lowest-income group. This "middle class" generally, considering the relatively high percentage of college-age youth from this income group that goes to college, does quite well in the proportions of public subsidies that it receives. Greater equity can be achieved through a reasonable redistribution of subsidies. A policy of low tuition by itself does no good for a student who cannot afford to go to college even at low tuition.[5]

The basic responsibility for equalizing opportunity should be carried as a public cost, and particularly at the federal level, and not as a cost assessed against individual institutions of higher education or against other students. Greater responsibility for these costs by the federal government (and by the states) would do much to ease the financial problems of many private institutions that tend to run their heaviest deficits in the student-aid area. We believe that these costs, in all equity, should be borne by the public at large and not by private institutions or by fellow students.

The general effort, however accomplished, should be to do less for those who now benefit most and to do more for those who now benefit least.

(4) *An increase in subsidies to institutions in the private sector* without injuring the public sector. Graduates from private colleges and universities make the same contributions to social benefits as do those from public colleges and universities. Private colleges and universities also provide a substantial proportion of the diversity that marks American higher education. They are now, however, threatened by the growing tuition gap between public and private institutions. Many of them have reached a peril point in their financing. This should be a source of great public concern.

We believe that the states should increasingly support private

---

[5] See Hoenack (1971).

institutions in ways that best preserve institutional independence, and that also make possible, in particular, the attendance of more students from low-income families. We especially favor aid through students in order to help preserve the independence of the private institutions and to increase the options open to students. We favor comparatively greater aid to low-income students so that they may have a better chance to attend private colleges if they so desire and so that the private colleges may have a student body more balanced among income classes—they should not be forced into becoming "class-status" schools nor should low-income students be impelled to go only to public institutions. Clear class-stratification between private and public institutions would be quite unwise.

Thus we prefer that states make tuition grants to students in accordance with their ability to pay. Federal funding of the State Incentive Grants program in the Higher Education Act of 1972 would encourage the states to embark upon or expand such programs. As such programs are introduced or extended, low-income students can be given a better chance to attend college and can have more options between public and private institutions open to them. At the same time, private institutions can be assisted in obtaining larger enrollments, meeting their costs, and getting a more balanced student body.

Only the states can gear together tuition policies at public institutions and tuition grants to students attending both public and private institutions. The states, and only the states can construct effective programs in these areas. Also, the states, and not the federal government, should take basic responsibility for *institutional* welfare within higher education.

Situations vary greatly from state to state in the proportion of students in private and in public institutions, and in other ways. There are, also, a number of alternative means of aiding private institutions. While we believe that tuition grants to lower-income students are a preferred device both for aiding such students and for the institutions they choose to attend, we also believe that there should be considerable diversity and experimentation among the states.

Private institutions must recognize that the more public funds they receive, the more accountable they will be held by public authorities. It is not likely to be possible to get subsidies on an "arbitrary amount" basis with no formulas for the amount and no reporting on its use. Private institutions must be prepared to consider methods of accountability along with methods of public funding.

Private institutions do, of course, now receive some indirect public subsidies, as well as some direct help from the federal government and from some of the states. Tuition on the average covers about three-fifths of educational costs, gifts and endowments about one-fourth, and direct public contributions about one-sixth. All of the direct public contributions and about half of gifts and endowments (because of forgone taxes) are a burden on public sources. Also, private institutions of higher education, along with public ones, do not pay property taxes and usually do not pay local assessments for public services, and parents of dependent students receive a personal income tax deduction. Thus, perhaps, the direct and indirect public subsidy is already 25 to 30 percent of the educational costs in private institutions. The public subsidy of public institutions is, however, more than 80 percent, since tuition covers less than 20 percent of educational costs.

The suggestions we make would greatly aid private institutions by (a) public assumption of more of the costs of student aid, (b) narrowing the gap between private and public tuition levels, and (c) providing tuition grants to lower-income students or in other ways assisting private colleges.

6   We make these additional suggestions:

▪ Tuition in private colleges and universities is likely to continue to rise, as it has historically, at about the rate of the rise in per capita disposable personal income[6] (a rough measure of rising ability to pay) or preferably at a somewhat slower rate; that it should rise faster than this in public colleges and universities until it reaches the level of about one-third of the educational costs of institutions as compared with the current one-sixth, in order (among other reasons) to narrow the tuition gap; and total student aid should rise sufficiently so that no one now going to college will be denied the opportunity because of rising tuition and so that others who cannot now go for financial reasons be

[6] See O'Neill (1973). Over the past few years, it has risen faster than this historic rate. It is unlikely this will happen in the future, however, because of the increasing competition for students.

able to attend. *We are opposed to any increase in tuition at public institutions except as such increases are offset by the availability of adequate student aid for lower-income students.*

We do not suggest that tuition at public colleges rise, even in the very long run, to the full amount of the educational costs of institutions, but rather that it might rise to about one-third of institutional educational costs, roughly in keeping with a division of total economic costs, two-thirds to students and parents and one-third to public sources and philanthropy as discussed above. This calculation assumes that all forgone earnings are included in total economic costs.

If public tuition were to rise to around one-third of educational costs, this would considerably narrow the gap with private tuition, which now offsets about three-fifths of the educational costs at private institutions. This does not imply that private tuition would then be less than twice as high as public tuition. (It is now on the average about four times as high at the undergraduate level.) The ratio would be more like $2\frac{1}{2}$ to 1, since educational costs at private institutions are higher by about 15 percent than at public institutions. This proposed adjustment, however, would substantially reduce the ratio that now exists. We believe the resulting gap in tuition would be both reasonable and viable. The historic ratio has been about 3 to 1, but the dollar gap in absolute terms is, of course, greater as costs rise and the absolute differences in tuition are important as well as the ratio.

We suggest that public tuition be set at about one-third of educational costs as a *general* rule, subject to adjustments for a low-tuition policy in public community colleges, for possible special consideration to Ph.D. candidates, and for other particular situations.

We regret the necessity of recommending any rise in public tuition, but (a) public tuition has been lagging behind private tuition very considerably in recent times, (b) greater equity in treatment between high- and low-income students requires some rise in tuition for those who can pay as well as more subsidies for those who cannot, and (c) public tuition is less of a burden on many families than it once was as the general level of incomes has risen. Also, many private institutions now have an excess capacity that will only be used as they appear more attractive to students on a comparative basis, including tuition costs. Additionally, the competition between public and private institutions is now too heavily based on price considerations alone. Both systems would benefit if the competition were based more on quality of effort.

It will take some time for public tuition to rise to one-third of educational costs without departing too greatly from recent developments. Public tuition has risen over the past five years at a rate 20 percent faster than the rate of increase in per capita disposable income during the period 1960 to 1972. If this faster rate of increase of tuition were to continue, and if educational costs were to rise at the same rate as per capita disposable income (which is the long-term tendency), it would take a very long time (well into the twenty-first century!) for public tuition to reach one-third of educational costs. To reach the one-third figure in one decade (1983) would take a rise of up to twice the rate of increase in per capita disposable income (or an increase of about 10 to 12 percent per year in tuition if per capita disposable income were to rise 5.8 percent per year as it did from 1960 to 1972).

Our views about tuition take into account the fact, set forth later, that the "real" cost of tuition (adjusted for general inflation) has remained stable for 40 years, while the "real" cost of public subsidies has tripled during this same period of time.

- Tuition should vary by level of education and thus by level of costs—less at the lower division than at the upper division and less at the upper division than at the graduate level. Costs at these levels now run on the ratio of about 1 to $1^1/_2$ to 3 or more, but tuition is more nearly 1 to 1 to 1 in many institutions. We do not mean to suggest—quite the contrary—that lower-division education *should* cost less than upper-division education. We only note this as a current fact. We strongly favor, instead, a major redistribution of resources into lower-division teaching. Currently, however, lower-division students pay a higher proportion of their total educational costs than do upper-division or graduate students. They are, in some situations, actually subsidizing the more advanced students. We especially favor low tuition at the lower-division level so that students may be given a better chance to get at least this much higher education and to try out their interests in academic life—they are often quite undecided at this stage. We do not favor a comparatively high tuition barrier against getting started in higher education as compared with continuing in it; such a barrier is more likely to discourage low-income than high-income students.

We particularly favor raising comparative tuition at the graduate level because of (a) the higher costs at this level, (b) the growing surplus of Ph.D.'s, (c) the greater opportunities of graduate students to support themselves as teaching assistants, as research assistants, and in other ways, (d) the comparatively high incomes for those who enter professional fields, and (e) the reality that many of the "externalities" or social benefits from higher education in political and social behavior will have been developed at the undergraduate level, if they are developed at all, and will not be increased much by graduate study. We recognize, however, that graduate schools are in great competition for the best students, and that this tends to drive down the price charged to graduate students as compared with the price charged to undergraduate students. Also, faculty members in universities with graduate students tend to prefer graduate to undergraduate students. The setting of policies for graduate tuition is an exceedingly complex matter. Situations vary greatly as among the M.A. level, the Ph.D. level, the several professional fields, and in other ways.

Overall, we believe that tuition should be more nearly proportional to costs, rather than regressive as against students at the lower levels. Thus we favor separately determined tuition levels for

The associate in arts degree

The B.A. and M.A. degrees

The Ph.D. degree

Other advanced professional degrees.

- A much improved national loan program should be developed. Students will increasingly assume more financial responsibility for themselves at earlier ages for several reasons, including reaching their majority at age 18. With more "stop-outs" for young persons and more "recurrent" education for older persons, the average age of students may rise (it is now 25 in the California community college system), and students will have higher costs because of greater family responsibilities. Public subsidies are likely to decrease in the long run as incomes rise, as less comparative educational deprivation must be overcome among segments of the American population, and as all remnants of deficits of highly trained manpower tend to disappear. Thus, other sources of income will need to be found. If both parents and the public come to feel less financial responsibility, the students will need to assume more responsibility, and an effective loan program will be necessary to make this possible. In any event, some greater charge to the users as compared with nonusers seems both equitable and inevitable in the long run—currently about one-third of adults are or have been users of subsidized higher education, and two-thirds are not and have not been.

The current national loan program has at least four major disadvantages—it does not provide for major or even for catastrophic risks, it is subject to a heavy default rate, it forgives rather than postpones interest while the student is in college, which can encourage undue short-term borrowing, and it makes no special allowance for the nonworking wife in a lower-income family. A better loan program is an urgent necessity.

7 We suggest funding in terms of major accounts as follows:

Basic research by government, mostly federal, and by philanthropy on the merit of individual projects.

Auxiliary enterprises by charges to the users.

Service activity by charges to the users, where possible, and by the appropriate level of government, where not possible.

Student aid basically by government—primarily the federal government—and by philanthropy.

Teaching by a combination of tuition, adjusted through state tuition grants for ability to pay; of philanthropy; and of government support, primarily state and local. We do not consider it to be either wise or necessary for the federal government to assume responsibility for basic institutional support for teaching in its totality.

Net forgone earnings by the users, with subsistence costs met through student aid on the basis of need.

Loan programs provided basically by the federal government with provision for full repayment, over variable periods of time as related to income, by the individual borrowers except in very special personal circumstances.

8 We cannot answer the very basic question of whether total economic costs of higher education are matched or more than matched by the total benefits. Institutional costs of higher education now account for about 2.5 percent of the GNP. If recent trends continue, this percentage will run to 3.3 percent in 1980. We have suggested elsewhere (*The More Effective Use of Resources*, 1972) that this percentage can be held to 2.7 percent without loss of quality while increasing equality of opportunity. There is no known way to prove whether more or less than this percentage of the GNP should be spent on higher education as compared with each and all of the other ways the GNP might be spent. The suggested figure of 2.7 percent for 1980, however, appears reasonable in our general judgment about the allocation of resources.

Were it possible to determine scientifically what percentage of the GNP should be spent on higher education, however, it would not be possible within the American system to do much about it. Our economy is not totally planned with a central budget that is disaggregated. Instead, expenditure patterns are aggregated from myriad individual and group decisions. Parents and students decide how much tuition they are willing to pay and how much money they are otherwise willing to spend for educational purposes. Federal agencies decide how much research they want. Donors decide how much money they want to give. States decide on what subsidies they wish to provide. A very large number of decisions are made by a very large number of people, and they add up to a certain percentage of the GNP. The real question is, then, whether the decision-making processes are generally good ones—do the right people have good enough information to make the right decisions under the right circumstances for the right reasons? We generally accept the decision-making processes now in effect, with the one major exception that we favor gradually more reliance on the market choices of students.

9 No "equal and exact justice" is possible, however desirable, in the distribution of the costs of and benefits from higher education. Among other reasons, the problems are too complex and the available data too inadequate. We are concerned, however, that a greater approximation to justice could be achieved if the changes we recommend were put into effect, and we believe they should be given a high order of priority. The directions, as we see them, are:

A short-term increase in the public share of monetary costs for education to be followed by a long-term increase in the private share until it again reaches about current proportions

A redistribution of the governmental burden from the states and localities toward the federal government

A redistribution of student subsidies from higher- to lower-income groups

A greater amount of support for private colleges and universities

A comparative, although modest and gradual, rise in public as against private tuition

A reevaluation of tuition policy to gear it more to the actual costs of education by level of the training

Greater reliance on better loan programs in the longer-run future and on charges to users

Careful conservation in the use of resources to minimize the rising impact on the GNP

We also are concerned that the totality of funds available to higher education be adequate.

The recommendations we make in this report are aimed at these results. (For a schematic outline of most of these recommendations see Table 1.) These recommendations should be considered all at once, and no one recommendation should be taken out of the context of this total additive approach to financing—for example, the raising of tuition without an increase in student aid.

This series of recommendations reflects some hard choices in the contest among groups of people and institutions for comparative preferment. We have favored in our proposals:

A larger public and a smaller private share of monetary outlays for education on a temporary basis in order to make possible greater equality of educational opportunity

A greater comparative burden on the federal government as compared with the states and localities

A greater advantage to lower-income and a lesser advantage to higher-income students

TABLE 1 *Suggested directions of movement in financing higher education, 1973 to 1983*

	Actual 1973	Proposed 1983
Percentage of the GNP expended on institutional costs of higher education	2.5	2.7
Private share of monetary outlays on education, in percentages	37.0	34.0
Governmental and philanthropic share of total monetary outlays on education, in percentages	63.0	66.0
Federal share of total governmental costs for higher education, in percentages	42.5	50.0
State and local share of total governmental costs for higher education, in percentages	57.5	50.0
Percentage of student subsidies that are "replacements" of private funds	66.0	33.0
State support of private institutions, or for students attending them	35 states	50 states
Percentage of educational costs at private institutions met by tuition	60.0	60.0
Percentage of educational costs at public institutions met by tuition	17.0	33.0
Ratio of private to public tuition at the undergraduate level*	4.0 to 1†	2.5 to 1
Tuition policy as related to cost by level of instruction	Generally equal tuition regardless of level of costs	Tuition geared more to costs by level of instruction
Loan programs	Moderate emphasis	Greater emphasis and substantial improvement in terms

*Costs at private institutions now average 15 percent higher than at public institutions. This percentage will rise somewhat as the mix of students in public institutions shifts in the direction of community and comprehensive colleges.

†The ratio is 4.9:1 when comparing charges for typical in-state undergraduates in public institutions and comparable charges at private colleges and universities; based on total FTE enrollment in the public and private sectors, however, the ratio is 4.3:1.

A more competitive tuition situation for private as compared with public institutions

A greater consideration for lower-division as compared with upper-division and graduate students in tuition policy

Not everybody can be comparatively better off in every way at the same time. The issues at stake are very substantial. We are considering here the means of financing one of the most important series of services in American society.

10   We recognize that, at some point in the future, the United States may need a more drastic overhaul of the financing of postsecondary education than we suggest here. However, the steps we do suggest are essential and, we believe, they can and should be undertaken now.

History has given us a very complex system of financing postsecondary education and one that is also deeply embedded in legislation and in expectations; thus it is not easy to change. Concern about this system of financing, however, has greatly increased in recent years and we expect that the level of this concern will be maintained and perhaps even heightened in the future. Factors at work include:

The increase by nearly $2^1/_2$ times in a single decade in the percentage of the GNP being spent on institutional costs of higher education—from 1960 to 1970.

The greater concern for equality of opportunity to attend college, and also for current inequities in subsidies between those who do and those who do not go to college. As more and more young people do go to college, these imbalances in subsidies will become both more serious and more publicly evident.

The battle among the federal, state, and local governments over the responsibility for financing programs in the area of human welfare.

The higher proportion of enrollments in institutions under public control. The system of higher education was once largely private, and financed more by philanthropy and less out of the public purse. It is now largely public and becoming more so.

The perilous financial condition of some private colleges.

The rising standard of family income that creates greater general ability to pay. Also, the demand for higher education is income elastic—it rises faster than incomes rise, and incomes keep on rising.

The emancipation of youth with its reduced sense of dependence on family guidance and support, and a concomitant potentially reduced sense of responsibility by parents and other adults. Achievement of legal majority at age 18 is a social factor of very great potential significance. Among other things, it can change the definition of who is a resident of a particular state, with great implications for in-state and out-of-state tuition levels.

The changing labor market that finds fewer deficits and more surpluses of academically trained persons, and thus creates less national need for constantly increasing enrollments.

The continuing tensions between the "adversary culture" followed by some persons on campus and large elements of the public.

The increasing element of *consumption* in a college education—(1) more current attention to personal enjoyment on campus through a more responsive environment and (2) more preparation for an interesting life, as through training in the creative arts. *Consumption functions* are inherently more of a private concern than are *production functions*.

Economists who once neglected this area of financing are now studying it with more and more depth and perception. More highly trained analysts are at work within federal and state agencies dealing with the financing of higher education.

Thus we have a complicated and embedded system of financing of postsecondary education, but one that is now subject to major and continuing pressures. It is highly unlikely that these pressures will not result in some major changes. Consequently, the financing of higher education will and should remain on the agenda for continuing examination for the foreseeable future. Any report on it, as a consequence, must be *interim* in nature, as is this one. Basic questions will be under discussion for a long time, not only about where we would like to be but also about how we get from here to there. We set forth in this report our current views of where we are, of where we think we should be, and of how we should manage the transition between the two.

2. The Educational Accounts

It is an obvious, but often obscured, fact that *people* pay the total bill for higher education—directly through charges to students and their parents, indirectly through tax assessments, through philanthropic gifts and bequests, through contributions to other institutions (for example, the church, foundations) that in turn support collegiate education. In these various forms and through these agencies, the current burden is shared among users and nonusers, the well-to-do and the less well-to-do, older and younger generations.

The principle of pluralistic forms of support for higher education in the United States is deep-rooted and historic, although the pattern of support has changed significantly over the years, and is undergoing further modification today. In the first two centuries after the founding of Harvard College the burden of college costs was shared principally between the family and the church. In the last century, support through public agencies—chiefly the state, which has the power of taxation—has come to play the most important role, and private philanthropy has also grown as a significant factor. There is, however, probably more questioning and controversy today than ever before concerning who should pay the bill for higher education. This is partly attributable to the rising level of public concern about equality of opportunity, and partly due to the increasing magnitude of the bill for higher education as college entrance has become a common experience for a majority of the nation's youth. Prior to World War II, public expenditures averaged about $300 for each student enrolled in higher education; today the public subsidy per student is about three times as large in real terms (up by a factor of seven in current dollars).

TABLE 2		
Public expendi- tures on higher education (in millions of dollars)	1939–40	$ 216
	1949–50	1,082
	1959–60	2,608
	1969–70	10,830
	1971–72	13,140*
	1980	20,000†

* Estimated.

†Projection.

SOURCE: Appendix A, Tables A-2, A-3, A-8, A-13; and projection by Carnegie Commission staff.

A family may pay only minor attention to economy and efficiency in budgeting small expenditure items in its household, but these issues become of paramount importance when a significant fraction of expenditures must be committed. When higher education was traditionally a privilege for the few and was largely financed by private funds, and when the lack of college education was not a significant barrier to job opportunities, public bodies paid little attention to who paid for and who benefited from collegiate education. Today, however, over two-thirds of all young men and women in the United States avail themselves of some type of formal postsecondary education, about half of the direct costs are paid from public revenues, and the rise of "credentialism" has made more evident the equity issues of inclusion in or exclusion from good job opportunities. Who does pay for higher education has become a subject of more serious review and analysis in recent years, and who ought to pay for it is an increasingly important issue of public debate.

It is useful to distinguish among several aspects of college costs. First, there is the nominal *price* charged for attending college—that is, the basic tuition and fees charged to each student. Interinstitutional comparisons are often made on the basis of this price, and the division of higher education in the United States into private and public sectors with different pricing philosophies frequently focuses attention on this basic element of the cost of attending college.

Second, there is the *out-of-pocket cost* to the student or his family, which includes tuition and fees, room and board (either as a resident student or a commuter), books and supplies, travel and other living costs, and which may be partially offset by scholarship grants. Thus the *cost* of attending even a tuition-free institution can be considerable to the student and his family. Conversely, the student with sufficient grants-in-aid may find even a high-tuition college inexpensive to attend.

Third, the cost of educational services in almost every institution of higher learning is subsidized. Subsidies come primarily from public funds in the case of public colleges and universities, although some of these institutions also have significant income from private gifts and endowments. Private institutions of higher education receive relatively more of their subsidies from endowments and from current gifts from alumni and friends, but they also receive public subsidies in the form of student aid and research and training grants. Both public and private institutions also receive subsidies in the form of property tax exemptions and special tax treatment of gifts. In considering national policy on matters of equity, the distributional (or redistributional) effects of these subsidies are important.

Finally, there are forgone income opportunities for the student, in many cases decisive in whether a person can or should attend college. A clear expense is involved on the part of the individual who gives up a job to go to or to return to college; there is an *opportunity cost* (in the language of the economist) for the individual who selects college rather than employment upon graduation from high school.

"Who pays for college education?" cannot be answered simply without giving attention to each of these aspects of cost. The fairness and effectiveness of our system of higher education must be viewed in a broad context if wise determination of public policy is to be made and implemented. Decisions by local, state, and federal governments must be concerned with the total cost to society of providing educational services, because choices among various social programs and objectives can only be made reasonably if the implications of alternative choices are discernible.

Perhaps the simplest way of viewing the question of "who pays?" is to take three different perspectives: from the vantage point of the *user*, from the perspective of the institutions providing educational services, and from an aggregative view of the educational system and the economy as a whole.

	Source of institutional income	Public institutions	Private institutions	Total
TABLE 3 *Aggregated institutional income accounts for higher education, 1970–71 (in millions of dollars)*				
1.	State government	6,610	110	6,720
2.	Local government	884		884
3.	Federal government			
	a. Research and service	1,180	1,280	2,460
	b. Other	1,000	330	1,330
4.	Tuition and fees	1,887	2,963	4,850
5.	Endowment	70	430	500
6.	Gifts	330	830	1,160
7.	Sale of services	105	38	143
8.	Related activities	1,190	1,120	2,310
9.	Student-aid income			
	a. Public sources	378	197	575
	b. Private sources	101	172	273
10.	Auxiliary enterprise	2,010	1,460	3,470
11.	Total institutional funds	15,745	8,930	24,675 (100%)
12.	Less: noneducational income	− 4,669	−3,947	− 8,616
13.	Total educational funds of institutions	11,076	4,983	16,059 (100%)

SOURCE: Computed by Carnegie Commission staff, based on O'Neill (1973). (See Appendix A.)

Before looking at the costs of higher education from these three perspectives, however, it is useful to simplify the educational accounts, as usually reported, to eliminate items that do not reflect the educational mission of colleges and universities. Too often, arguments concerning educational costs or benefits are based on data that are misleading or confusing. Tables 3 and 4 attempt to consolidate and simplify the educational accounts, illustrating alternative ways of measuring the cost of higher education.

Lines 1 through 13 of the first three columns of Table 3 show the typical form of reporting institutional income by broad classifications. The four right-hand columns indicate the sources of these funds by the category of payer.

Family	Taxpayer	Philanthropy	Other
	Burden of costs borne by:		
Family	*Taxpayer*	*Philanthropy*	*Other*
	6,720		
	884		
	2,460		
	1,330		
4,850			
		500	
		1,160	
			143
			2,310
	575		
		273	
3,227			243
8,077	11,969	1,933	2,696
(34.6%)	(48.5%)	(7.8%)	(9.1%)
−3,227	−2,420	−273	−2,696
4,850	9,549	1,660	
(30.2%)	(59.5%)	(10.3%)	

Several classes of income must be deducted to obtain a clearer picture of the purely educational operations of educational institutions. These are federal research and services, sale of services, related activities, student-aid income, and auxiliary enterprises.

FEDERAL RESEARCH AND SERVICES About three-fourths of federal payments to colleges and universities for research and services are for activities that could have been performed by other contractors and which are not an integral part of the educational process. One-fourth of such funding is assumed to be basic support of education in which research is a *joint product* with the teaching function. Although this division is somewhat arbitrary, it reasonably accurately reflects

TABLE 4 Consolidated institutional income accounts and total economic costs of higher education, 1970–71 (in millions of dollars)

Source of income or expenditure	Public institutions	Private institutions	Total	Burden of costs borne by:		
				Family	Local, state, and federal	Philanthropy
State and local	7,494	110	7,604		7,604	
Federal	1,295	650	1,945		1,945	
Tuition and fees	1,887	2,963	4,850	4,850		
Endowment	70	430	500			500
Gifts	330	830	1,160			1,160
Total educational funds of institutions	11,076	4,983	16,059	4,850 (30.2%)	9,549 (59.5%)	1,660 (10.3%)
+Student subsistence				6,299		
−Student aid*				−3,084	+2,383	+ 321
Total monetary outlays on education			21,978 (100%)	8,065 (36.7%)	11,932 (54.3%)	1,981 (9.0%)
+Forgone income (net of student subsistence)				16,859		
Total economic cost			38,837 (100%)	24,924 (64.2%)	11,932 (30.7%)	1,981 (5.1%)

*Student-aid income to families is greater than the sum of student-aid expenditures by government and philanthropy by virtue of institutional grants-in-aid paid from current funds. See Appendix A, Table A-14 for the derivation of the student-aid estimates.

SOURCES: Table 3; and Appendix A, Table A-14, and estimates by Carnegie Commission staff.

the proportion of research funds that would have to be provided from some source to provide the same level and quality of education. In fact, it is likely that university-sponsored research, on balance, has societal benefits that outweigh the public and private costs of conducting that research. This issue is discussed more fully in Appendix B.

SALE OF SERVICES Services provided for fees under this category primarily include services performed for nonstudent audiences. This amount is deducted in the summary account in Table 4.

RELATED ACTIVITIES

Income from this source generally includes fees for extension programs, athletic and artistic events, operation of real estate, and a variety of other income categories that are not essential to the main educational function of institutions. While some portion of this income comes from students for extracurricular activities, this item is removed in the summary account as being primarily income from noneducational activities.

STUDENT-AID INCOME

Student-aid funds pass through institutions, coming from public or philanthropic gifts or grants and are passed on to students to enable them to pay for tuition and subsistence expenses. Thus to leave student-aid income in the educational income account would be to double count it as institutional income. In 1970–71, colleges and universities had student-aid income from public sources totaling an estimated $575 million, plus $273 million from private sources. In the same year student-aid expenditures by institutions of higher education were an estimated $1,228 million, the excess above reported income coming from current general funds. In Table 3, student-aid income is deducted from total educational income, but student-aid expenditures are shown in the lower section of Table 4 as an offset to family expenditures. More detailed information on sources of student-aid funds is provided in Appendix A, Table A-14. Loans are not included because they represent revolving funds, but estimated public subsidies in the form of forgiven interest while students are in college are included.

AUXILIARY ENTERPRISES

Income from the operation of dormitories, cafeterias, and bookstores is eliminated in Table 4 so as not to double count when student subsistence costs are later added as a family cost. Ordinarily income from this source is almost evenly balanced off by expenditures, leaving the auxiliary accounts as essentially "wash" items in the institutional income and expense accounts.

The above adjustments are illustrated by contrasting Table 3 with the upper portion of Table 4. In the revised, shortened, form only income from fees, government, and from philanthropy are included, for these are the essential sources of support for the educational activities of institutions. Appendix A describes these adjustments more fully and provides a picture of changes in the nation's higher educational accounts from 1929–30 to 1969–70 in more detail.

In the following sections the definitions of the cost of higher education, as presented in Table 4 (and Appendix A), are used consistently throughout. A brief glossary of terms may provide a useful guide.

GLOSSARY OF TERMS   The following terms will be used in analyzing the costs of higher education:

Institutional funds   Those amounts of money that pass through the accounts of individual institutions during the fiscal year. As measured here, it is the total income received by institutions of higher education for all educational and noneducational purposes.

Educational funds of institutions   Expendable funds received in the fiscal year that are designated for educational support or are unrestricted as to use; determined by deducting from institutional funds those items that were received for noneducational services (for example, for dormitories, cafeterias, sale of services to nonstudents, real estate property, sponsored research).

Monetary outlays on higher education   Educational funds of institutions plus living and incidental expenditures paid by students and their families (net of student aid received) plus payments directly to students from government or philanthropic agencies for student assistance. This measure avoids the double counting of student-aid funds that would be involved if expenditures by institutions, families, and government agencies were merely summed.

Economic costs of education   The sum of monetary outlays on higher education plus the lost earnings (net of subsistence costs) of students occasioned by attending college rather than taking full-time employment. This measure provides an estimate of the economic alternatives forgone by reason of college attendance.

Forgone income   An estimate of what students could have earned in full-time employment had they entered the labor force instead of college. It is estimated by multiplying the number of full-time-equivalent students enrolled in higher education times the average weekly earnings of 18- to 21-year-old high school graduates in the labor force, times 40 weeks of employment, minus an allowance for estimated unemployment (assumed to be twice the overall national rate).

Educational subsidies Funds provided from either public or private sources to reduce the cost of education to the student. In public colleges and universities, the student typically pays tuition that meets only a small proportion of his cost of education. The remainder is provided chiefly by direct appropriations of the state government. In private colleges and universities, the student typically pays a larger proportion of his cost of education, but some of it is subsidized from institutional endowment funds and gifts. Student-aid funds, whether from public or private sources, are also granted to students to meet all or part of their tuition.

See Appendix A for further discussion of these categories and their derivation.

3. An Aggregate View of College Financing

The American economy has been devoting an increasing percentage of its total resources to higher education since World War II. As Table 5 indicates, the share of educational expenditures in the GNP has approximately tripled over the last 15 years. It seems likely that this share will continue to increase until about 1975, and then will remain relatively constant over the next decade as expected total college and university enrollments stabilize. The Commission's report on *The More Effective Use of Resources* (1972) recommended a target expenditure level (in terms of "total current expenditures," as in Column 4 of Table 5) for higher education in 1980 of $41.5 billion in 1970 dollars, or 2.7 percent of the anticipated GNP.

Viewed in the aggregate, the costs of higher education are shared by individuals as *users* (students and their parents), by taxpayers, and by private philanthropy. But there are several alternative ways, each appropriate in its own context, of looking at the consolidated financial account of higher education. Table 4 illustrated these alternative measures for 1970–71.

The first three columns of Table 4 show the chief components of income for educational purposes received by institutions of higher learning. The three right-hand columns, and the adjustments in the lower portion of Table 3, attempt to provide a more meaningful cost classification for the discussion of who pays for higher education.

The distribution of the burden of costs in the right-hand columns distinguishes among family costs associated with college attendance, taxpayer costs at the local, state, and federal level, and philanthropic contributions, including income from past gifts held in the form of endowment. In 1970–71, about 30 percent of educational income received by institutions came from

Higher education: Who pays? Who benefits? Who should pay? **30**

TABLE 5
Expenditures
from current
funds by
institutions of
higher education,
and gross
national product
(in billions of
dollars)

Year	GNP (1)	Expenditure on student education (2)	Education and general expenditure* (3)	Total current expenditure† (4)	2/1 (5)	3/1 (6)	4/1 (7)
1955	398	2.2	2.8	3.5	0.55	0.70	0.88
1960	504	3.6	5.1	6.3	0.71	1.01	1.25
1965	685	6.8	9.9	12.4	0.99	1.45	1.81
1970	974	14.0	19.7	24.2	1.44	2.02	2.48

*Includes organized research and related activities expenditures.
†Includes expenditures for auxiliary enterprises and student aid.
SOURCES: U.S. Office of Education (1966, 1972b).

students and their families, 60 percent came from governments, and 10 percent from private philanthropy.

The cost of attending college, however, is both more than is shown in the income received by institutions by virtue of living costs of students and expenses for books, supplies, etc., and less than is shown by virtue of sizable student-aid grant funds. In 1970–71, these grant funds were particularly large as a result of educational benefits for Vietnam veterans. These adjustments are shown in Table 4, resulting in a figure that includes all of the basic monetary outlays by students and parents, taxpayers, and private philanthropy for higher educational services in 1970–71. In this balance of accounts it can be seen that families contributed approximately 37 percent of the net total, governments contributed 54 percent, and private gifts accounted for 9 percent.

Before getting into the more controversial subject of forgone income as a cost of higher education, it may be useful to look at how the sharing of college costs has changed over time. Appendix A provides tables for selected years between 1929–30 and 1969–70, showing a consistent series over the 40-year period. Charts 2A and 2B show the trends over time for educational funds of institutions and total monetary outlays on higher education. Clearly the pattern changed rather sharply at the time of World War II, when government funds began to play a substantially larger role than previously. The postwar increase in costs borne by the taxpayer was partly because tuition charges did not rise proportionately with educational costs in the public sector, but more importantly because the public sector has grown much more rapidly than the private sector over the last

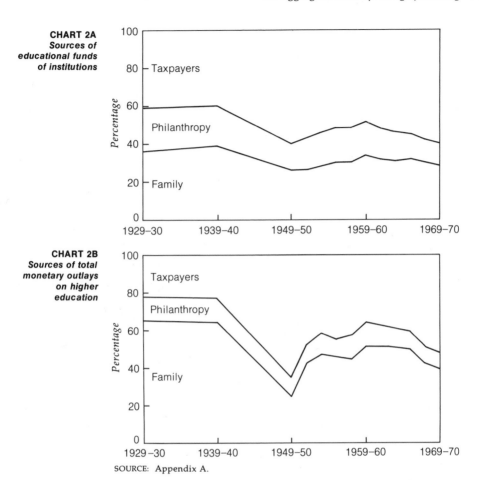

CHART 2A
*Sources of
educational funds
of institutions*

CHART 2B
*Sources of total
monetary outlays
on higher
education*

SOURCE: Appendix A.

25 years. The change is perhaps most marked in the total monetary outlay on education, since it includes substantial increases in student-aid funding principally from federal sources. 1949–50 was only a year after the peak of World War II GI benefits and 1970–71 again saw a sharp rise in veterans' educational benefits. Approximately 7 percent of total outlays for education in 1970–71 were in the form of veterans' educational benefits, as contrasted with only 2 percent in 1959–60, but over 15 percent in 1949–50.

Quite apart from the irregular impact of veterans' support, however, the trend over the last 30 years is clear. The contribution by students and their families has declined significantly (if one eliminates veterans' benefits, the decline has been from 64 percent of the total outlay in 1939–40 to 35 percent in 1970–71), and taxpayer support has risen dramatically (from 23 percent to 55 percent). Philanthropy's relative share has dropped by one-fifth.

Table 6 gives a somewhat more detailed picture for the family contribution since 1929–30. Total charges against students and their families have increased twentyfold in the period while total enrollments have increased sevenfold. Student aid, however, has increased markedly over the last few years, thus keeping the average family burden from rising significantly. Per student costs are illustrated in the lower half of Table 6, where it can be seen that improved student funding has significantly aided the average student. (Veterans' benefits accounted for 38 percent of all student aid in 1970–71.)

Table 7 and Chart 3 give a better comparative picture of the trend in average outlays per student, and the rise in per student subsidies (combined taxpayer and philanthropic subsidies). The most striking fact is that, while dollar outlays for higher ed-

TABLE 6 *Monetary outlays by students and parents for higher education, 1929–30 through 1970–71*

	1929–30	1939–40	1949–50	1959–60	1969–70
Total outlays ($ millions)					
Tuition and fees	$144.1	200.9	701.9*	1,161.8	4,330.0
Living and incidental costs	367.0	409.2	1,251.7	1,952.1	5,704.2
Total	511.1	610.1	1,953.6	3,180.6	10,034.2
Less: student aid (including veterans' benefits)	− 13.0	− 22.4	−1,054.3*	− 445.4	− 2,309.4
Net outlay	$498.1	587.7	899.3	2,668.5	7,724.8
Average outlay per student ($)					
Tuition and fees	163	173	325*	422	722
Living and incidental costs	415	354	580	705	951
Total	578	527	905	1,127	1,673
Less: student aid†	− 15	− 19	−489*	− 161	− 385
Net outlay per student	$563	508	416	966	1,288

*Payments of tuition and fees by the Veterans Administration directly to colleges and universities have been included both as tuition payments and as student aid to make 1949–50 comparable with later years when all payments were made directly to students.

† More than 90 percent of student aid consisted of veterans' benefits in 1949–50; 52 percent of aid in 1959–60 and 29 percent in 1969–70 came from this source. See Appendix A, Table A-14.

SOURCES: Appendix A, Tables A-1, A-2, A-3, A-8, and A-13; U.S. Office of Education (1972); and O'Neill (1973).

	Monetary outlays by family, per student		Higher educational subsidies per student	
Year	Current dollars	Constant 1967 dollars	Current dollars	Constant 1967 dollars
1929–30	$ 563	$1,097	$ 310	$ 604
1939–40	508	1,221	289	695
1949–50	416 (751)*	583 (1,052)*	1,015 (680)*	1,422 (953)*
1959–60	966 (1,050)*	1,107 (1,194)*	951 (867)*	1,088 (1,001)*
1969–70	1,288 (1,401)*	1,181 (1,294)*	2,029 (1,916)*	1,763 (1,650)*

TABLE 7
Per student family outlays for higher education, and per-student subsidies

* Figures in parentheses are computed by excluding veterans' benefits paid to students from student aid. Since student aid adjustments reduce family outlays and increase subsidies, outlays are greater and subsidies smaller when veterans' benefits are omitted.

SOURCE: Computed from Appendix A and the Bureau of Labor Statistics Consumer Price Index.

CHART 3
Family outlays and higher educational subsidies per student in constant (1967) dollars, 1930–1970

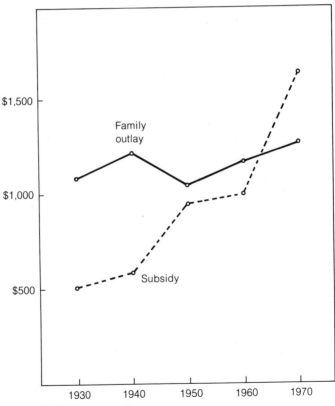

SOURCE: Table 7.

ucation on the part of the average student and family are three times as high today as they were 20 or more years ago, in real terms (after deflating for cost-of-living changes) the average cost of attaining higher education has remained almost unchanged for the last 40 years. This surprising constancy on the part of the *average* outlay is accounted for by the increasing proportion of students over the years attending low-tuition public institutions, and by the rapid growth of student assistance. The nonrepresentative student who attended a private institution without financial aid would have experienced an increase in the cost of attending college (including subsistence costs), in constant 1967 dollars, from about $1,000 in 1939–40 to about $3,000 in 1969–70. But he was more than compensated for by the larger number of his counterparts who attended public institutions and/or received student aid.

Prior to World War II, private gifts and endowment income accounted for approximately one-third of the subsidies in higher education. The GI Bill in the late 1940s substantially boosted the public contribution for several years, but in 1959–60, the two-thirds public–one-third philanthropic contribution had been reestablished. A dramatic shift has occurred in the last dozen years, however, and even though private support has tripled in absolute terms, it now accounts for only about one-seventh of the total subsidy to higher education (one-sixth if one omits Vietnam veterans' benefits). Between 1959–60 and 1970–71, public subsidies jumped from $1.96 billion to $12.0 billion, while the philanthropic contribution rose from $.67 billion to $1.98 billion.

4. Capital Costs

Tables 3 and 4 gave a picture of the consolidated current fund account for institutions of higher education; plant costs were excluded except for annual operating and maintenance costs. By 1966–67, according to June O'Neill's study (1973) for the Carnegie Commission, colleges and universities were adding to their total investment in capital stock at the rate of about 11.5 percent annually.

Table 8 shows the sources of plant fund income from 1949–50 to 1966–67. Over the 1957–1967 decade about 51 percent of plant income originated with state and local governments, 14 percent came from federal sources, 23 percent from private gifts and grants, and 12 percent from other institutional income.[1] The "other" category was about one-half from student fees, one-fourth from earnings on plant fund investments, and one-fourth from services and related income.

Table 9 estimates capital costs as a percentage of educational expenditures from current funds. Columns 3 and 4 provide an estimate of these additional costs based on annual plant fund income reported in Table 8. Columns 5 and 6 provide an alternative estimate made by June O'Neill (1971), using the sum of estimated depreciation of capital stock plus forgone interest. In periods of rapid expansion of facilities the annual plant-fund-income method produces a larger capital cost estimate than the less variable depreciation-and-interest method used by O'Neill. In a period of more modest expansion such as the 1970s is likely

---

[1] In addition to a plant fund income of $1,587.4 million in 1967, institutions borrowed $1,901.8 million. Approximately 70 percent of such borrowing was for auxiliary enterprises, and 30 percent was for academic facilities. Net borrowing, after repayments of principal, was approximately $1,310 million for the year.

TABLE 8
Plant fund income of institutions of higher education, by sources, 1949–50 to 1966–67 (in millions of dollars)

Year	State and local governments	Federal government	Gifts and grants	Other	Total
1949–50	303.3	12.4	72.6	79.9	468.2
1951–52	160.3	12.7	71.6	12.8	257.4
1953–54	146.9	8.4	103.9	32.8	292.0
1955–56	240.0	13.3	143.2	40.6	437.1
1957–58	421.8	63.0	157.2	54.8	696.8
1959–60	356.7	57.6	196.5	77.1	687.9
1961–62	551.4	70.5	226.5	104.5	952.9
1963–64	694.8	134.2	314.6	159.2	1,302.8
1965–66	820.0	333.7	366.1	376.4	1,896.2
1966–67	729.1	289.1	355.7	628.6	2,002.5

SOURCE: O'Neill (1973).

to witness, the O'Neill method would produce consistently higher capital cost estimates than those based on annual receipt of plant funds. Under either approach it seems appropriate to assume that annual capital costs add 10 to 20 percent to annual operating costs, probably ranging between 12 and 15 percent over long periods of time.

Returning to the 1970–71 figures for total institutional costs of education reported in Tables 3 and 4, an estimate for capital costs (estimated at 12 percent of current educational costs) can be

TABLE 9
Alternative estimates of capital costs as a percentage of current educational income, 1949–50 to 1965–66

Year	Plant fund income ($ millions) (1)	Percentage attributable to instructional purposes* (2)	Instructional plant fund income ($) (3)
1949–50	468.2	66.0%	309.9
1953–54	292.0	64.7	188.9
1957–58	696.8	65.1	453.6
1961–62	952.9	62.3	593.7
1965–66	1,896.2	63.8	1,104.6

*Estimated by taking educational income, as defined in Table 3, as a percentage of total institutional income.

†O'Neill's annual capital cost estimates (1971, p. 91) include estimated depreciation of plant and interest income forgone on plant investment. Annual costs are approximately 8 percent of the value of total capital stock.

SOURCE: Computed from Table 8 and Appendix A.

TABLE 10
Estimated edu-
cational and
capital costs, by
source of funds
1970–71 (in mil-
lions of dollars)

	Total	Family	Taxpayers	Philanthropy
Current educational funds received by institutions	$16,059 (100%)	4,850 (30.2%)	9,549 (59.5%)	1,660 (10.3%)
Additional capital costs*	$ 1,700 (100%)		1,253 (73.7%)	447 (22.3%)
Total annual costs	$17,759 (100%)	4,850 (27.3%)	10,802 (60.8%)	2,107 (11.9%)

*That portion of capital costs (12 percent) paid by student fees and other institutional income is omitted from the capital cost allocation so as not to double count; it is already included as income in the first line.

SOURCE: Carnegie Commission staff.

added to round out the picture. Table 10 gives this estimate, with capital costs allocated in proportion to the contribution of each income source in the 1957–1967 period. The effect of adding estimated annual capital costs is to raise total educational costs by about $1.7 billion for 1970–71, to raise the philanthropic contribution by 1.6 percentage points, and to increase the taxpayer share by 1.3 percentage points. The family share of the total cost burden declines from 30.2 percent to 27.3 percent.

In the remainder of this report attention is focused principally on current income and expenditures on institutions, but it should be remembered throughout that capital costs are an

Percentage of educational income (4)	O'Neill capital instructional cost estimate† ($ millions) (5)	Percentage of educational income (6)
19.8%	239.8	15.3%
9.8	357.6	18.6
14.9	497.7	16.4
12.8	646.8	13.9
13.5	1,043.7	12.8

additional element that must be taken into consideration when viewing higher education in its totality. Because capital costs are more difficult to estimate and to allocate appropriately, they are treated only in this brief section.[2]

---

[2] The reader is referred to the more detailed study of June O'Neill (1971) for further analysis of capital costs.

5. Considerations of Equity

One might reasonably ask whether the $14 billion of public and private funds in 1970–71 that subsidized higher education were effectively allocated to accomplish society's aims. The Panel on Financial Need Analysis of the College Scholarship System recently concluded that if all educational subsidies were equitably distributed in terms of financial need a significant step toward equality of opportunity could be made.

It seems clear that if it were possible to reconstitute the entire system of higher education, it could be done in such a way that all financial need of qualified students could be met today with existing resources. Within the framework of the present dual system, however, there seems little likelihood that such a goal could be accomplished within a reasonably short time without seriously crippling private or public institutions (College Entrance Examination Board, 1971, p. 7).

More than two-thirds of all support funds subsidize the *price* of higher education. Because many students from upper-income families attend institutions with tuition charges that are far below costs (true in the case of many private colleges and universities as well as public institutions), these educational subsidies are not distributed as effectively as might be the case if minimizing the financial barrier to attendance were the primary goal. For example, of the total monetary outlays on higher education, students and their families on the average contribute about 37 percent of the total ($8.1 billion out of $22.0 billion in 1970–71). National data on student financing are not adequate to indicate precisely the contribution by families in various income categories, but Table 11 is an approximation of

TABLE 11
**Estimated
percentage of
total monetary
outlays on
college
education met by
students and
parents**

Parental income quartile*	1970–71 contribution
Highest income quartile	52%
Second quartile	40
Third quartile	32
Lowest income quartile	24
Average	37

*According to A.C.E. national norms, based on freshman survey questionnaires, the parental income levels that divide these quartiles were approximately $8,500, $12,000, and $18,000. For all students, whose parents would average about three years older than the parents of freshmen only, these amounts should probably be increased by about 10 percent.

SOURCE: Estimated by the Carnegie Commission staff. See Appendix C.

the current pattern.[1] If the average family contribution remained unchanged, the only means by which education could be made nearly free for children of parents in the lowest-income quartile would be by a correspondingly larger contribution by families in the upper-income quartile.

In a diverse educational system in which approximately one-fourth of all college students attend private institutions, and in which pricing decisions for the public sector are made by various local, institutional, and statewide agencies within each of the 50 states, each with its own historical tradition, it will not be possible to alter the distribution of subsidies markedly within a short span of time. However, in the last quarter of this century, when a majority of the nation's youth are expected to attend college, it is reasonably certain that increasing pressure from the body politic will insist upon efforts to eliminate financial obstacles to college attendance for students from low-income families. It also seems likely, as college enrollments stabilize (or possibly contract modestly) in the 1980s, that the private sector will come under increasing financial strain if the tuition differential between public and private institutions widens further.

The Commission believes that both equity considerations

[1] Reasonably good data are available for California for 1971–72, indicating that the family contribution (student and parent) ranged from 38 percent for families with incomes below $6,000 to 55 percent for families above the $18,000 income level (California State Scholarship and Student Loan Commission, 1972). See Appendix C for a more detailed analysis by educational sector and family income level.

and emerging problems of retaining vitality in private higher education call for a serious reexamination of the distribution of the burden of college costs. Quite apart from the question of the relative contribution by "users" and taxpayers, which will be discussed in other sections of this report, the Commission urges that attention be given to this distributional problem at both the national and state levels. State governments should be primarily concerned with issues of pricing policy in public institutions and the possible partial subsidization of educational costs at private institutions (which are alternative or complementary ways in which tuition differentials may be narrowed). But state governments should also be concerned to some degree with assistance to low-income students, even though we believe the federal government should assume the primary responsibility for student aid. Federal policy will concern itself not only with programs to aid the disadvantaged, but also with regional equalization of educational resources and the support of specific areas of study (e.g., medicine, science) in which a vital national interest is involved. The Higher Education Act of 1972 is an important step by the federal government in the recognition of its role in assuring more equitable access to higher education.

Robert Hartman has analyzed the likely impact of the Basic Educational Opportunity Grants program under the Higher Education Act of 1972, and has estimated that some 500 thousand to 1 million additional students might be induced to attend college if the basic grants were fully funded (Hartman, 1972*b*, pp. 465–496). The costs of the program would range from approximately $1.9 to $2.5 billion, with a large proportion of the aid going to students in the lowest family income quartile. (The costs would be reduced somewhat after allowing for the impact of the ceiling on the proportion of a student's costs that can be covered, to be discussed in Section 14.) If fully funded, the effect of this major new federal program would be to reduce the average contribution of the lowest income quartile families (see Table 11) to about 10 percent and would lower the contribution in the third quartile to about 20 percent.

6. The Tax Burden

The taxpayer contribution to the support of higher education, as shown in Table 4, amounted to approximately $12 billion in 1970–71, or 54 percent of the total monetary outlay.

One would have to make heroic assumptions to estimate the incidence of that share of taxes that goes to pay for higher education. However, certain general conclusions can be drawn. Approximately 60 percent of tax funds supporting higher education come from state revenues, about 8 percent from local government taxes, and 32 percent from federal sources. Local tax structures are almost invariably regressive, depending chiefly upon real estate and sales tax sources. State tax burdens are, on balance, nearly proportional to income above the lowest income brackets. In some states, which rely heavily upon sales and excise levies (e.g., Connecticut and New Jersey), state taxes have a regressive impact. The federal tax structure relies on the progressive personal income tax for about 60 percent of its revenues (over and above social insurance), and so its burden is moderately progressive throughout the range of taxable incomes.

Data on federal tax returns show the following effective rates of taxation for federal income taxes and for other taxes which are deductible on federal income tax returns. The latter are predominantly state income taxes, state and local sales taxes, and local property taxes, and thus give a reasonably good picture of the burden of state and local tax systems.[1]

[1] The real burden of state and local taxes is likely to be more regressive than indicated because of the imposition of many taxes (excise and property) at intermediate levels not perceived by the taxpayer but reflected in the price (or rent) of such expenditure items. However, if one takes into consideration public transfer payments under various forms of public assistance, the net regressive impact is considerably moderated.

	Income group	Federal income tax	Other deductible taxes	Combined effective rate
TABLE 12 *Effective tax rates by income group; federal income tax and other taxes deductible for federal income tax purposes, 1970*	Under $3,000	4.3%	10.7%	14.5%
	$3,000–$5,000	8.4	8.2	15.9
	$5,000–$7,500	9.5	7.3	16.1
	$7,500–$10,000	10.9	7.1	17.2
	$10,000–$15,000	12.0	7.0	18.2
	Over $15,000	18.8	7.0	24.5

SOURCE: Computed from U.S. Internal Revenue Service, *Statistics of Income, 1970, Individual Income Tax Returns.*

From census data, the distribution of the college-age, 18- to 24-year-old, population by family income group can be estimated as shown in column 2 of Table 13. The actual percentage of the eligible population currently or recently enrolled as undergraduates varies from 23 percent for the lowest income group to 66 percent for the $15,000-and-over income group. The rate of graduation from high school also varies directly with family income level.

The proportion attending public institutions, not unexpectedly, varied inversely with family income level; 86 percent of

TABLE 13 *Income distribution of all families, families of the college-age population, and families of college attenders, fall 1971*

Family income	All families	Families of college-age population (18 to 24 years of age)	Families of college attenders†	College attenders as percentage of 18- to 24-year age group
Total number*	49,070	20,185	8,030	
Total percentage	100.0	100.0	100.0	39.8
Under $3,000	9.8	8.4	4.8	23.0
$3,000–$5,000	13.6	13.7	9.2	26.7
$5,000–$7,500	17.9	20.2	14.4	28.3
$7,500–$10,000	18.2	18.5	17.6	38.0
$10,000–$15,000	24.6	22.8	26.7	40.6
Over $15,000	15.8	16.4	27.2	66.1

*Total excludes families not reporting income.

† According to census data, approximately 65 percent were currently enrolled, 12 percent had completed college, and 23 percent had completed one to three years of college but were not currently enrolled.

SOURCE: U.S. Bureau of the Census (1972, Table 13).

students from the lowest income group were in public institutions compared to 66 percent from the over-$15,000 class (see Appendix D, Table D-2).

These data also provide the basis for an estimate of the distribution of taxpayer subsidies for undergraduate education by income group. Table 14 shows the distribution by family income of the college-age population, of the tax contribution required to provide higher educational services, and of institutional subsidies from tax funds. Column 2, showing the estimated distribution of the direct tax burden, gives a one-to-two weight to federal income taxes and to "other deductible taxes" to reflect the approximate one-third federal–two-thirds state and local government contributions to the support of higher education.

Table 14 suggests that income groups up to the $10,000 level contribute a smaller share of tax funds than the share of benefits they receive in the form of institutional subsidies from tax sources. Proportionate tax burdens and subsidy benefits almost balance for families in the $10,000–$15,000 range. Above $15,000 the effect of the progressivity of tax rates is evident. If approximately $3 billion in student aid funds from tax sources were added to institutional subsidies, the low-income and lower-middle-income groups would apparently further increase their share of total benefits.

Reviewing the distribution of institutional subsidies, several counterforces are evident. Upper-income level families are represented by a high proportion of students (35.5 percent) in

TABLE 14 Income distribution of families of college eligible population, estimated tax burdens, and benefits from tax-funded institutional subsidies, 1971			
Family income group	Families of college-age population (1)	Tax burden (2)	Institutional subsidies (3)
Under $3,000	8.4%	2.1%	4.8%
$3,000–$5,000	13.7	5.6	8.7
$5,000–$7,500	20.2	10.4	13.3
$7,500–$10,000	18.5	14.0	17.7
$10,000–$15,000	22.8	26.5	27.5
Over $15,000	16.4	41.4	28.0
TOTAL	100.0%	100.0%	100.0%

SOURCES: Tables 12, 13, and Appendix D.

public universities, where per student subsidies are considerable, and by a low proportion in public two-year colleges (10.8 percent), where the subsidies are relatively low. For the $3,000-and-under income group these percentages respectively are 21.2 percent and 34.1 percent. On the other hand, a considerably higher percentage of upper-income youth attend private colleges and universities (34.5 percent), where tax-funded subsidies are relatively less important, than do the lowest income group (13.6 percent). Thus the estimated distribution of tax-funded institutional subsidies in Table 14 does not differ greatly from the distribution of attendees by family income level, as shown in Table 13 (column 3).

If it is judged merely in relation to estimated tax contributions, the distribution of institutional subsidies by family income appears to contribute to greater social equity.[2] But if one contrasts the distribution of these subsidies with the family income distribution of the college-age population, one might arrive at the contrary conclusion. The lowest income groups have a larger share of such dependents (8.4 percent) than the share of higher educational benefits they receive (4.9 percent), while the over-$15,000 group receives an estimated 27.6 percent of subsidy benefits for its 16.4 percent of the 18- to 24-year-old age group. The system works moderately well to aid those who attend college, but significant obstacles to entrance still exist. Not all of these are financial, but the necessary financial outlay and the sacrifice of earnings from alternative use of one's time and energies is obviously a serious constraint for many young persons.

It should also be recognized that data on public subsidies do not include certain relatively hidden public subsidies, such as the tax exemption of cash gifts and the exemption from capital gain of gifts in the form of securities or real property. These subsidies tend to go predominantly to relatively selective colleges and universities, increasing the share of all public subsidies benefiting relatively middle- and upper-income families.

No calculation of taxpayer contributions to and benefits from higher education at a single moment in time, however,

---

[2] This conclusion applies to the overall national data, but it may not apply equally in all states and regions. Hansen and Weisbrod (1969) have argued the reverse in a study of California in the mid-1960s, although there has been a lively controversy in interpreting their findings. See p. 90 below.

provides an adequate basis for judgments about equity. Typical taxpayers begin their working lives in relatively low-income jobs, and as their children grow up, their incomes rise until late middle age, when income normally falls again. Thus, the lowest income groups at any moment in time are disproportionately populated with elderly persons and young workers who do not yet have children of college age. Different income groups receive different mixes of tax-supported benefits, and while middle-income groups may receive more in higher educational support, lower-income groups probably receive more in public assistance, Medicare, and so on. One would need to have data on lifetime incomes and lifetime public benefits before drawing firm conclusions about the social equity of any given pattern of costs and benefits.

Many aspects of the public support of higher education may be considered in the light of redistribution in addition to those by income class. Families without children make approximately the same tax contribution as those who directly benefit by sending children to college; families with children not of college age share the burden at any moment in time with families who have children attending college; single taxpayers likewise contribute to the education of their neighbors' children through approximately the same tax contribution as do families who directly benefit from sending their children to college.

The major redistributive influence, however, appears to be intertemporal. Families contribute taxes throughout their working lives, but receive benefits in a relatively concentrated period of time—when their children are of college age. If one looks at the total educational system from kindergarten through college, however, this unevenness in the balance of costs and benefits is sharply diminished, for parents receive substantial benefits from public education at the elementary and secondary school level earlier in their working careers.

7. Forgone Income

If a student gives up or delays taking an income-producing job to go to or return to college, he or she obviously has an additional cost of attending college over and above actual expense outlays. For some students (or potential students) this is a major factor in determining attendance, and it should be considered a cost of attending college.

Economists who have been concerned with rates of return on the investment in human capital ordinarily have attempted to estimate forgone income as a "cost" for all students. In terms of a person's lifetime stream of earnings, the choice to go to college postpones earnings in the hope of adding to potential earnings in the future. These "opportunity costs" are correctly included if one is primarily concerned with comparing rates of return on various types of private and social investment. And it could be argued that any *rational* decision concerning college attendance would be made with at least some awareness of forgone alternatives.

In an unpublished staff paper for the Carnegie Commission, Walt McKibben estimated forgone incomes for college students (undergraduate and postbaccalaureate) for 1966. Average hourly wage rates for employed high school graduates between the ages of 18 and 24 were used as a base, and the weighted hourly wage rate so determined was 93 percent of average hourly earnings in manufacturing. This percentage has been used to adjust earnings in manufacturing in the calculations below for other years. Forty weeks was taken as the typical period of time claimed by the academic year. In fact, the normal academic year requires only about 34 weeks in residence, but few students are able to find employment during short holidays or interterm vacations.

Estimates of annual forgone income per student have been reduced by 12 percent to allow for actual average earnings by students during the school year (see Schultz, 1971, p.111), and assume that the average unemployment rate for students of college age was double the national average for all members of the labor force. (For those without a college education, unemployment rates in the 18- to 24-year-old age group average $2^1/_2$ to 3 times the overall rate.) Table 15 shows gross forgone earnings for 1929–30 to the present, and forgone income net of subsistence expenditures. (The latter figures appear in Table 4 and tables in Appendix A, because subsistence costs are already included in total monetary outlays on education.)

As indicated in Table 4, the inclusion of net forgone income as a cost of education to the student and his family adds significantly to the total estimated cost of education. Table 16 gives some perspective on the changing relative importance of the major items of cost visible to the family. Since World War II, not only have the numbers of students increased dramatically, but also the labor market now accommodates nearly full employment and a gradual compression of income differentials between young, relatively unskilled workers and their older coun-

	Gross forgone incomes		Forgone incomes net of subsistence costs*	
Year	Per capita ($)	Total ($ mill.)	Per capita ($)	Total ($ mill.)
1929–30	$ 562	$ 495‡	$ 190	$ 167
1939–40†	521	604‡	161	188
1949–50	1,492	3,615‡	957	2,063
1959–60	2,347	6,517	1,620	4,498
1970–71	3,668	23,104	2,676	16,859

TABLE 15 *Estimated forgone income of college students, 1929–30 to 1970–71*

* Subsistence costs for 1970–71 were estimated to be approximately $1,000 (about $1,200 for residential students on campus, and $850 for students living off campus—predominantly at home). Estimates for other years have been made by adjusting this per capita figure for changes in the consumer price index.

† The estimated unemployment rate for 1939–40 was 31 percent for college-age nonstudents, as compared to rates ranging from 11 percent to 13.8 percent for the other years. Thus, the "opportunity cost" of attending college was relatively low during the Depression years.

‡ T. W. Schultz's estimate (1971, p. 85) for 1950 is $3,781 million, $802 million for 1940, and $560 million for 1930. The appreciable difference in the estimates for 1939–40 is due largely to different assumptions regarding the unemployment rate.

SOURCE: Estimates developed by Carnegie Commission staff.

TABLE 16 *Tuition and fee charges, subsistence costs, student aid offsets, and net forgone incomes as percentages of total family economic costs of higher education*

	1929–30	1939–40	1949–50	1959–60	1969–70
Tuition and fees	23.0	25.8	16.3*	16.2	18.4
Subsistence costs	58.7	52.6	51.6	27.2	24.3
Less: student aid	−2.1	−2.9	−43.5*	−6.2	−9.8
Net forgone incomes	20.4	24.4	75.6	62.8	67.1
TOTAL	100.0	100.0	100.0	100.0	100.0

*In 1949–50 all tuition payments made by the Veterans Administration to private institutions, and one-half of the cost-of-education allowances paid to public institutions, have been included both as tuition and fee charges and as student aid. It does not appear that veterans' benefits seriously distorted the tuition charges of private institutions, but the cost-of-education-allowance paid to public institutions was considerably greater than normal tuition.

SOURCES: Compiled from Appendix A, Tables A-1 through A-13; and O'Neill (1973); and estimates by Carnegie Commission staff.

terparts, so that the forgone earnings opportunities during college attendance have become more costly. By contrast, as a percentage of total economic cost (including forgone income), direct tuition and fee charges and student subsistence costs have declined significantly. Subsistence costs were once *the* major cost of college attendance; today they amount to little more than tuition charges and are overshadowed by forgone incomes.

Although the inclusion of forgone income is appropriate for certain types of analysis of college costs—and it is a very real cost to the student who must give up a job to complete college—for other types of considerations it may not be relevant. For the typical parent who supports a son or daughter through college, the choice may be between paying for college costs, or having the son or daughter become an independent economic unit. Thus no income to these parents is forgone—they merely would be relieved of subsistence costs if their child did not attend college, and these costs are already included in the estimate of monetary outlays for college attendance.

Similarly, forgone income is not a major factor in the short-run calculation of costs for many students from relatively affluent families. In these cases, the alternative to entering college may not be an immediate job, but travel, public service, or the enjoyment of leisure time in the final years of maturing into adulthood. But for students from low-income or from lower-middle-income families, forgone earnings are likely to be viewed as a significant sacrifice. This is especially true in families in which the earning power of the family head has been impaired by disability or frequent unemployment, or in low-income families with several siblings of the potential student. In such cases the family may well suffer from giving up the contribution to total family earnings that a college-age family member would be capable of making. Thus, when we consider total economic costs, we find that the barriers to college attendance for young people from low-income families appear relatively more severe than in terms of monetary outlays alone. This is particularly important when considering the cost of attending a public community college, where tuition tends to be low—forgone earnings are an important sacrifice for the young people from low-income families who form a larger proportion of students in these colleges than in four-year institutions.

From the longer historical perspective, the interesting point is that the average family share of the total monetary outlays for higher educational services has declined over the last 40 years from nearly two-thirds to nearly one-third (see Chart 2B); however, when forgone incomes are included, as Chart 4 indicates, the family share of the total cost has remained relatively constant at about two-thirds of the total. Greatly expanded student aid programs, particularly during the years when veterans' benefits have been large, have tended to diminish the monetary share paid by students and parents, but, simultaneously, in-

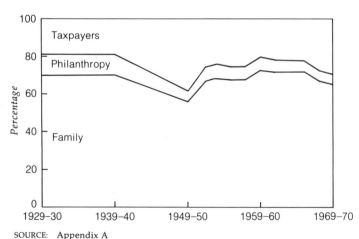

CHART 4
Share of total economic costs of education (including forgone income) borne by taxpayers, philanthropy, and family

SOURCE: Appendix A

comes forgone by virtue of attending college instead of entering the work force have increased sufficiently to offset this and stabilize the overall private share of the cost burden.

Forgone incomes may be a "real" cost of attending college for a minority of students—in the sense of representing a barrier to attendance—but they are also important in the broader context of determining the appropriate pattern of long-term investment in human capital for the benefit of society in general.

8. Tuition as Income to Institutions of Higher Education

Tuition and fee charges are a significant source of income to institutions of higher education. As Table 17 indicates, however, tuition income has declined from 34 percent of total educational income prior to World War II to about 30 percent today. State and local contributions have increased significantly in relative importance over the past 20 years, although perhaps not as much as one might have expected in light of the growth of enrollments in the public sector. Federal funds to support institutional programs (as opposed to student-aid support) are only now approaching the 15 percent level. Private philanthropy—gifts plus endowment earnings—has steadily declined as a percentage of income over the last 40 years.

Over the last ten years, partly as a result of the more rapid rate of increase in tuition charges, both public and private institutions have increased their outlays for student aid substantially. Student aid is not shown separately in Table 17, because part of it is included in the gross tuition and fee income shown in the table. At a later point, we shall present data on net tuition and fee income—gross tuition after deduction of the portion of student-aid income that is used by students to meet their tuition and fees.[1]

When tuition rates increase, there are always internal pressures to increase scholarship funds at least by an absolute amount equal to the tuition increase for students receiving grants-in-aid. In addition, most institutions have intensified their efforts to be more representative of the population in their student mix. Thus, student-aid expenditures have risen from

[1] Some student aid is also used for subsistence expenses, but these expenses also do not appear in Table 17.

TABLE 17 *Educational income of institutions of higher education,* by source of funds, 1929–30 to 1969–70*

	1929–30	1939–40	1949–50	1959–60	1969–70
State and local government	39.8%	33.3%	35.3%	41.1%	45.0%
Federal government	2.0†	7.4	25.8 (6.2)‡	11.7	14.7
Tuition and fees	35.1	38.1	25.2 (44.8)‡	31.3	29.9
Endowment earnings	16.7	13.5	6.1	5.6	3.1
Gifts	6.4	7.7	7.6	10.3	7.3
TOTAL	100.0%	100.0%	100.0%	100.0%	100.0%

* Excludes income for sponsored research, auxiliaries, and services to nonstudent groups.

† Estimated.

‡ Figures in parentheses count $307.3 million paid directly to institutions by federal government for World War II veterans as tuition and fees.

SOURCE: Appendix A.

4.1 to 8.0 percent of operating costs for public institutions, and from 10 to 14.8 percent for private institutions. As a percentage of gross tuition income, the increases have been from 18.8 to 34.9 percent for the public sector, and from 14 to 21.6 percent for the private sector.

However, a significant portion of these expenditures is funded from public sources (for example, economic opportunity grants, work-study) and from private gifts, grants, and restricted endowment earnings. Table 18 shows the sources of funds for student-aid expenditures for public and private institutions in recent years.

Student-aid funds, administered by institutions but coming from public (predominantly federal) sources, have increased most rapidly over the last six years. This total can be expected to continue to rise if the Higher Education Act of 1972 is adequately funded. Contributions by institutions themselves out of current general funds have nearly tripled in this 6-year period. Aid from private gifts, grants, and endowment earnings have lagged behind these other sources. As several recent studies have indicated (Jellema, 1971; and Cheit, 1971), a significant part of the financial difficulty faced by colleges and universities today is attributable to increases in student aid, both to offset the effect of tuition increases on low- to moderate-income students and to encourage admission of disadvantaged students. This is particularly important in explaining the deficits of private colleges and universities.

TABLE 18
*Sources of
institutional funds
for student aid
expenditures,
public and private
institutions,
1965–66 to
1971–72 (in
millions of
dollars)*

		Funded from		
	Student aid expenditures	*Public sources*	*Private sources*	*Current funds*
Public institutions				
1965–66	156	81	42	34
1967–68	332	209	55	68
1969–70	480	300	80	100
1971–72	760*	475*	125*	160*
Private institutions				
1965–66	273	40	100	133
1967–68	387	121	119	146
1969–70	520	170	150	200
1971–72	700*	230*	200*	270*

* Estimated.

SOURCE: Appendix A, Table A-14.

Part of the problem facing institutions of higher education in determining their tuition levels and student-aid policies is that the portion of total scholarship aid over which they have direct control is relatively small. For 1971–72 all forms of student aid (excluding loans by banks and public agencies)[2] for all levels of higher education are estimated in Table 19.

[2] Federally insured loans for 1971–72 were approximately $1.18 billion.

TABLE 19
*Estimated
student aid funds
expended in
1971–72 (in
millions of
dollars)*

Sources of funds	*Amount*
1. *Current general funds of institutions*	$ 430
2. *Institutionally administered, from gifts, grants, and endowment income*	325
3. *Institutionally administered, from public agencies*	705
4. *State scholarship programs*	280
5. *Federal payments directly to students*	2,275
6. *Private scholarships, paid to students*	50
TOTAL	$4,065

SOURCES: Table 23 and estimates developed by Carnegie Commission staff (see source references to Table A-14).

Category 1, representing less than 10 percent of the total, is the only one over which institutions have complete discretion. Category 2 is in some cases restricted as to allocation, but can ordinarily be used with a reasonable degree of freedom. Category 3, principally funds from the U.S. Office of Education and largely for disadvantaged students, is highly restricted as to use but generally complements institutional financial aid goals. Categories 4, 5, and 6 are usually known to the colleges and universities if the recipients request other aid or must be certified as bona fide students, but the great bulk of these funds (e.g., over $2 billion in veterans' and social security payments) are not based solely on need. They are, however, *related* to need, for families of social security beneficiaries (chiefly widows' and survivors' families) tend to have low incomes, and most veterans could probably qualify for assistance on the basis of need. Over the next several years, as veterans' assistance declines and strictly need-based *entitlement* funds increase, institutions may be aided substantially by the federal government in attempting to erase financial barriers to attendance.

For institutions of higher learning, when other sources of income are insufficient to meet rising costs and obligations, tuition fees are often the only source of income to which they can turn. Thus private institutions, for whom tuition income represents about 60 percent of funds expendable on education (Table 4), have increased tuition charges rapidly in response to rising costs, while income from gifts and endowments has increased more slowly. For the past two or three years, public institutions have increased tuition charges more rapidly than per student costs have increased, mainly because state governments have been under increasing pressure from competing claimants for state revenues. When the pressure to get into college was greater than the number of available places, it was a relatively simple matter to pass on cost increases to students and their families. Today, however, an increasing number of private colleges and universities are experiencing declining enrollment, and even many of the high prestige institutions are finding that they must go much deeper into their pool of applicants to maintain the size of their freshman classes. Some public institutions have also experienced a drop in students, and students are becoming more vocal in their opposition to fee increases without compensating improvements in student aid.

Looking to the near future, it seems likely that the attention of college and university administrators, trustees, and legislatures will be forcibly drawn more to efforts to control costs and thus to minimize the need for sizable annual tuition increases. However, as the new federal basic opportunity grants to low-income students are funded, state legislatures may feel less constrained to keep public tuition levels low, knowing that even the poorest student can afford to contribute significantly. Under the final compromise language of the Higher Education Act of 1972 such grants cannot exceed one-half of the actual cost to the student, thus requiring matching financial aid from other public or private sources for the low-income student. Some observers have interpreted the new federal program as indirect revenue sharing, with federal funds assuming one-half of the initial contribution to student costs for students with financial need, and state funds becoming supplementary. Such a development would tend to narrow the tuition differential between public and private institutions, and work to maintain the share of private education, at least in absolute numbers, and perhaps in percentage terms.

The Commission sees the entrance of basic federal student funding as a new force in higher education that may alter familiar attitudes toward tuition policies. It will be possible for colleges and universities—especially the traditionally low-cost public institutions—to impose somewhat higher tuition without barring access to low-income students. However, we believe that any changes should be gradual, and that a disservice would be done if state legislatures attempted to "capture" these federal funds by a rapid escalation in public tuition charges. As we have stated in several earlier reports, we believe that, particularly for lower-division years of college, students should have available a satisfactory quality low-cost college option. We should not ignore the fact that even commuting students in community colleges have significant cost outlays over and above tuition charges,[3] and that an escalation in such charges would impose considerable hardship on students from

---

[3] The California State Scholarship and Loan Commission (1972) survey of student-aid resources in 1971 found that students from families with less than $6,000 income spent, on the average, $700 on college costs over and above tuition from self-help sources (one-fifth from parents, and four-fifths from earnings and loans).

low-income and lower-middle-income families. But, over the period of a decade or longer we would consider it a healthy move if, as direct student support becomes more broadly and equitably available, the tuition gap between public and private institutions narrows once again. In the absence of major state or federal programs of institutional aid to private colleges, this can only come about by a somewhat more rapid increase in public tuition levels than has occurred in the past. We see such a trend as desirable only if an increasing fraction of those charges is being supported by federal grants-in-aid to students, thus gradually shifting a rising portion of the burden of college costs to the federal government with its broader and more progressive tax base rather than to the student or parent from an already low-income group.

9. User Costs for Higher Education

Services in the American economy are usually provided either by private initiative, with prices set to cover the costs of providing those services, or by public initiative with full or partial subsidy from public revenues. Services that are determined to be socially necessary and that are felt to have social benefits greater than the sum of individual benefits are frequently provided by the public sector. In the evolution of our society, education has gradually shifted from being a predominantly private activity, toward becoming part of the public sector. This transition was begun in the early nineteenth century for the grammar schools, was extended to secondary education in the first quarter of the twentieth century, and is increasingly becoming the dominant pattern for higher education in the second half of this century.

There are few other sectors of American society where private and public institutions exist side by side, and although this tolerance for (even encouragement of) diversity is beneficial in many ways, it also creates stresses and strains. The clear dividing line between the public and private collegiate institutions, moreover, has become increasingly blurred over the years, and we are developing a mixed system that has few parallels in other parts of the world or of contemporary American society.

In periods of relatively stable prices and only modest growth in enrollments, tuition charges in the public and private sectors maintained a reasonably constant relationship to one another. As Charts 5A and 5B indicate, throughout the 1930s tuition charges at private colleges were about three times as high as they were in the average public institution. In the immediate postwar period the gap narrowed considerably (chiefly because

CHART 5A *Average tuition charges in public and private institutions per FTE student, 1929–30 to 1972-73*

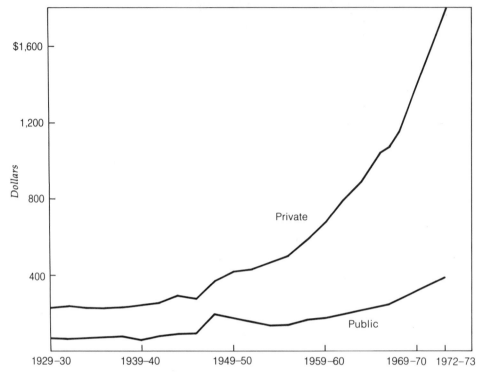

SOURCE: O'Neill (1973), updated by Carnegie Commission staff.

the majority of male students were returning veterans whose tuition was paid for under the GI Bill), and only returned to its prewar level in 1953. Over the last 15 years, however, and most strikingly in the period of rapid expansion in enrollments and general cost inflation, representative tuition levels have drawn farther apart. This partly reflects the greater willingness of the states to absorb a substantial portion of the increase in cost for public higher education (as contrasted with the private institutions, which have experienced an erosion of the real contribution of endowment and gift income). The tuition difference also partly reflects the changing "mix" in the public sector, as the proportion of two-year colleges, typically maintaining low tuition charges, has expanded relative to public senior institutions. By 1971–72, average gross tuition and fees of private institutions were 4.9 times those at public institutions (Table 20).

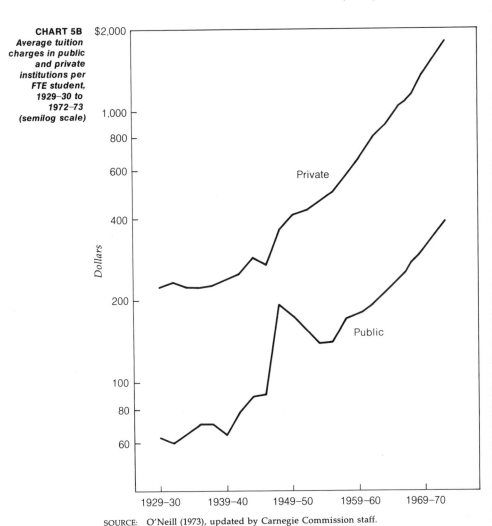

CHART 5B *Average tuition charges in public and private institutions per FTE student, 1929–30 to 1972–73 (semilog scale)*

Private

Public

1929–30 1939–40 1949–50 1959–60 1969–70

SOURCE: O'Neill (1973), updated by Carnegie Commission staff.

The ratio was even higher for two-year colleges. When board and room charges are taken into account, the ratios are considerably lower, because board and room charges at private institutions tend to exceed those at public institutions by relatively modest margins. Even so, total charges for residential students tend to be more than twice as high in private as in public institutions.

Between 1960 and 1972 the following average annual percentage increases in tuition were recorded, compared with increases in per capita disposable income, and in the consumer price index:

Disposable income per capita	5.8%
Average tuition charge per FTE student	
Public institutions	5.3%
Private institutions	6.9%
Consumer price index	2.9%

TABLE 20   *Gross tuition and fee charges and total charges for residential students, by type and control of institution, 1961–62 to 1971–72*

Type of institution and year	Tuition and fees			Total charges, including board and room		
	Public*	Private	Ratio private/public	Public	Private	Ratio private/public
All institutions						
1961–62	$218	$ 857	3.9	$ 869	$1,666	1.9
1965–66	258	1,154	4.5	983	2,004	2.0
1969–70	320	1,516	4.7	1,197	2,518	2.1
1971–72	367	1,781	4.9	1,349	2,906	2.2
Universities						
1961–62	265	1,059	4.0	947	1,882	2.0
1965–66	327	1,369	4.2	1,106	2,317	2.1
1969–70	413	1,794	4.3	1,342	2,903	2.2
1971–72	483	2,105	4.4	1,527	3,354	2.2
Four-year colleges						
1961–62	182	838	4.6	788	1,570	2.0
1965–66	240	1,086	4.5	903	1,898	2.1
1969–70	309	1,470	4.8	1,145	2,434	2.1
1971–72	365	1,740	4.8	1,305	2,820	2.2
Two-year colleges						
1961–62	88	490	5.6	599	1,198	2.0
1965–66	109	769	7.1	671	1,559	2.3
1969–70	187	1,065	5.7	956	2,065	2.2
1971–72	224	1,285	5.7	1,098	2,441	2.2

* Tuition and fees shown here are for in-state students. Out-of-state charges average about three times those for in-state students.

SOURCE: U.S. Office of Education (1972b, Table 44).

The widening differential in tuition charges is even more evident if one views the tuition income per student after the subtraction of student aid provided by the institutions themselves. Table 21 illustrates the trend over the last 16 years. The average net tuition income per student in the public sector has increased about 90 percent in 16 years—the increase has been highest in the two-year colleges (which started from a low base), and least in the universities—while in the private sector the increase has averaged 190 percent. The ratio of net tuition income per student between private and public institutions rose from 2.9 to 1 for the university sector in 1953–54 to 4.5 to 1 in 1969–70, and from 4.1 to 1 to 5.3 to 1 in the four-year colleges. In the two-year college sector the ratio had regained approximately its 1953–54 level after a sharp increase in the late 1950s. But, for all institutions, the ratio of net tuition in the private sector to that in the public sector was 5.1 to 1 in 1969–70 (the latest year for which such data are available), as compared with a ratio of 4.7 to 1 for gross tuition.

Perhaps even more important than the ratio of tuition levels, in the minds of most parents, is the absolute dollar difference. In terms of net tuition charges per FTE student, the gap had grown from $302 in 1953–54 to $967 by 1969–70 for universities, from $295 to $900 for four-year colleges, and from $249 to $782 for the two-year colleges.

This widening gap in tuition charges has clearly been important in the decline in the share of total degree-credit enrollment held by the private colleges and universities. As Table 22 indicates, the rate of decline in enrollment share has accelerated since 1960.

Even in the moderately high-tuition private college or university, however, tuition and fees represent only about 60 percent of the cost of attending a residential college. Room and board rates average about $1,000 today in public institutions and approximately $1,200 in private institutions, and incidental expenses add several hundred dollars to the minimal cost of attendance. In 1970–1972, average basic charges (tuition, fees, board and room) were $1,305 in public institutions and $2,820 in private institutions for the residential student.[1]

---

[1] Office of Education (1972*b*, Table 44).

TABLE 21
Net tuition
income per FTE
student, public
and private
universities,
four-year
colleges and
two-year colleges,
1953–54 to
1969–70 (in
dollars)

| | Public sector | | |
Year	Universities	4-year colleges	2-year colleges
1953–54	157	94	53
1957–58	177	105	69
1961–62	207	135	80
1965–66	257	182	115
1969–70	279	211	156
Percentage increase 1953–54 to 1969–70	78%	124%	194%

SOURCE: O'Neill (1973), updated to 1969–70 by Commission staff.

Students from families that can afford to pay substantial tuition and fees are more frequently found in the high-tuition private institutions.[2] The distribution of students by family income characteristics is positively correlated with tuition level, but the correlation is not high. While the public two-year and four-year colleges have to a considerable degree been developed to provide low-student-cost geographically-accessible opportunities for postsecondary education, the long-run interests of providing equal educational opportunity would not be served by a rigid stratification of student populations by socioeconomic status. Similarly, the high-tuition private liberal arts colleges may provide a unique environment for higher edu-

[2] Although, two-thirds of the college students from families with income in excess of $15,000 are enrolled in public institutions.

TABLE 22 *Degree-credit enrollment in all institutions of higher education and in private institutions, 1950–1970 (in thousands)*

Year	Total degree-credit enrollment (1)	Enrollment in private institutions (2)	Percentage in private institutions (3)	Five-year change (in percentage points) (4)
1950	2,281	1,142	50.1	
1955	2,653	1,177	44.4	−5.7
1960	3,583	1,467	41.0	−3.4
1965	5,526	1,902	34.4	−6.6
1970	7,920	2,120	26.8	−7.6

SOURCE: U.S. Office of Education (1972a).

	Private sector			Ratio, private/public			
Universities	4-year colleges	2-year colleges	Universities	4-year colleges	2-year colleges	Total
459	389	302	2.9	4.1	5.7	3.5
565	471	554	3.2	4.5	8.0	3.8
776	634	672	3.7	4.7	8.4	4.3
975	885	752	3.8	4.8	6.6	4.5
1,246	1,111	938	4.5	5.3	6.0	5.1
171%	186%	211%				

cation, but such colleges have not served only the well-to-do—nor would they wish to do so.

Taking the whole universe of higher education, grants-in-aid to students by the institutions themselves have increased more rapidly than have tuition levels. In 1953 the difference between gross and net tuition income was 13 percent; by 1971 it had grown to 27 percent.

Scholarship aid from institutional funds is awarded primarily on the basis of need, and so the bulk of such support aids students from low-income families. The average grant given to a typical recipient is several times as large as the average amount per full-time-equivalent student. For example, the average amount expended on student aid per full-time-equivalent undergraduate at Harvard in 1967 was $480, while the average award per aid recipient was $1,500 (tuition $2,000). At the University of Kansas the equivalent amounts were $40 per full-time-equivalent student and $325 per recipient (tuition $340).

In addition to institutionally administered funds, as we have seen, awards are made directly to students by the federal government (including, today, approximately $1.5 billion in GI educational benefits and $0.5 billion through social security), by state scholarship programs, and by philanthropic agencies.

Federal support of undergraduate students for the last five years is shown in Table 23. It has increased by nearly $2 billion in this short period chiefly as the result of veterans' assistance and Office of Education student-aid programs. By 1972–73 over $3^1/_2$ million undergraduate students were being assisted with

Agency	1969	1970	1971	est. 1972	est. 1973
H.E.W.					
Office of Education	377	615	721	889	908
Social Security Administration	366	401	455	505	537
Health Agencies	21	33	39	46	46
Veterans Administration	429	539	1,068	1,459	1,560
Defense	*	*	85	97	100
N.S.F.	5	4	4	4	4
Justice and Other	*	*	17	24	32
TOTAL	1,225	1,675	2,389	3,024	3,187

* Not available.

SOURCE: 1971, 1972, and 1973 Federal Budgets.

federal funds, out of a total undergraduate enrollment of about $7^1/_2$ million. The average award was $640, and the estimated average amount received per grantee approximately $800 (some students were assisted by more than one program).

While student-aid funds have improved substantially over the last five years, and now total about $4 billion from all sources (Table 19), they are provided by a patchwork of agencies and institutions, each with its own sense of mission or responsibility. The Panel on Financial Need Analysis of the College Scholarship Service, in its review of the past 15 years, concluded:

A cherished myth of educators and the general public is that student financial aid today is primarily based on relative need. However, when the source and application of all aid funds (including the G.I. Bill, Social Security, athletic grants, and scholarships from restricted funds) are considered, the greater amount of student aid appears to be beyond institutional control and is commonly awarded on the basis of criteria other than need. . . .Thus, while the Panel is moderately critical of institutional practices as revealed in its study of a number of colleges and universities, it also recognizes that financial aid officers have the impossible task of attempting to complement, or compensate for, all the irregular (and sometimes inequitable) patterns built into the system of financing higher education (College Entrance Examination Board, 1971, p. 9.)

From its inception the Carnegie Commission has urged more adequate student-aid funding through a broad federal program of educational opportunity grants. We recommended that such grants, based on need, be at the maximum level—then proposed at $1,000 per year—for undergraduate students in the lowest income quartile, and at one-half of that amount for the second lowest quartile; we recommended modest supplemental aid for some students in the lower range of the third quartile (*Quality and Equality, Revised,* 1970c, p. 5). The Commission welcomes the inclusion of the Basic Opportunity Grants program in the Higher Education Act of 1972, believing that this is a signal first step toward an orderly restructuring of student assistance.

The Commission has consistently recommended the maintenance of low tuition levels in community colleges, and preferably a lower rate for lower-division students in public senior colleges than for the junior and senior years. It has also expressed concern that, if present trends continue, private colleges and universities will tend to price themselves out of the market. However, recognizing the cost-income squeeze affecting most institutions, the Commission has urged efforts to make more effective use of given resources on the one hand, and increased public support, including cost-of-education supplements, to partially offset increases in cost on the other. The Commission believes that the recommendations made in *The More Effective Use of Resources* (1972), if effectuated, could hold down the rate of increase of costs to approximately 2.5 percent per year in the 1970s above the general rate of inflation.

It seems clear, however, that the average "user cost" of higher education will continue to rise. Greater equity in the distribution of "user cost" can be achieved by narrowing the tuition gap between private and public institutions, and by channeling more student aid to lower-income students.

10. The Benefits of Higher Education

The benefits of higher education are of several sorts and accrue both to individual users and to society as a whole. Throughout the long history of advanced education it has been a doorway, although not an exclusive one, to a world of intellectual and aesthetic appreciation, and a path toward advantageous and sometimes privileged occupations. In the modern world of economic industrialization and political democracy, education has come to play a critically important role for society in helping to provide a source of inspiration, renewal, and innovation.

Some of these benefits are quantifiable, and attempts have been made in recent years to measure the pecuniary benefits both to individuals and to society. Other benefits are more subjective, having to do with the development of the human personality and intellect, or with the creation of conditions that enhance the nature and organization of society. In asking "Who benefits from higher education?" each of these effects must be taken into account.

RATES OF RETURN ON THE INVESTMENT IN HUMAN CAPITAL Over the past dozen years, following in the footsteps of Theodore Schultz of the University of Chicago, economists have devoted considerable energies to attempts to measure the return on investment in human capital. Both the individual and society at large must choose between investment in the education of individuals or alternative forms of investment that may have a more discernible rate of return. To make rational decisions, it has been argued, the *yield* on investment in human capital should be known—because additional years of schooling can be presumed to add to the earning capacity of an individual in later life.

A human investment calculus can be made by taking the direct costs of education plus the forgone income (or output) resulting from college attendance rather than economic employment, and then comparing this sum with the discounted income stream that beneficiaries of education can expect throughout their lives. Comparing the average earnings associated with various levels of education in relation to the additional cost of obtaining that unit of education, one can estimate the rate of return for various segments of higher education.

Gary Becker's major study (1964) used detailed 1940 and 1950 census data to calculate average incomes of adults by educational attainment. He then calculated *private* rates of return by establishing the costs borne by students and their families, including forgone income, and *social* rates of return by adding in all educational subsidies. The relevant income streams were posttax income for calculating private rates of return, and pretax income for the equivalent rates for society as a whole. Becker estimated the private rate of return to be approximately 14.5 percent in 1939 and 12.7 percent in 1949 for white males. The rates of return for nonwhites were several percentage points lower. Social rates of return were 13 percent in 1939 and 12.5 percent in 1949. These yields were slightly higher than the customary 9 to 10 percent rate of return anticipated by investors in private business.

A number of more recent studies have been made; one of the most interesting is by Taubman and Wales (1972), which uses a sample of air force veterans for whom scores on the Armed Forces Qualifying Test (AFQT) were available, as well as follow-up surveys on education and earnings for 1955 and 1969. The AFQT data allowed the authors to test for interactions between ability, family background, schooling, and income. Compared with high school graduates with the same ability and family background, they estimate social rates of return of 14 percent for one to three years of college, 10 percent for baccalaureate attainment, 7 percent for some graduate education, 8 percent for the master's degree, and 4 percent for the Ph.D. They conclude that the lower rates of return at the graduate level indicate diminishing returns to additional education, but we would suggest that they may also reflect increasing components of nonpecuniary income for persons with advanced education.

Comparisons of changes in rates of return over time, and comparisons among nations, are instructive, but the use of such findings to make current decisions on investment in education either on the part of an individual or a society is subject to pitfalls. A number of conceptual and methodological issues are raised by these studies.

Assuming for the moment that measuring the pecuniary rate of return is a relevant calculation, a number of problems remain in assessing the accuracy of such measures. For example, it is assumed that social benefits are merely the sum of individual pretax benefits as measured by incomes earned after formal education. In the absence of quantifiable measures of external benefits, earnings are assumed to be equivalent to the productive contribution of individuals to society. Perhaps more importantly, differences in lifetime earnings between those with more and those with less education are assumed to be causally related to the educational experience. Attempts have been made in several studies to standardize for differences in ability and background, but other intangible qualities such as motivation and aspiration are omitted. One might reasonably ask, for instance, if—once a decision to attend college was made—a group of potential students who were given four years of travel, leisure, and independent study would produce an equivalent yield.

College may act as a screening device that identifies individuals with certain motivational qualities; it may separate out young men and women who have the determination and self-discipline to cope with additional years of study, and these same traits may be the determining factors in their later success in the world of work. In addition, credentials are becoming increasingly important because employers sometimes bar less-educated persons from occupations with better advancement potential on the assumption that a college education promises higher productivity. To the extent this is true, this is a quite appropriate judgment.

The young man or woman who wishes to make an educational and career decision based upon anticipated rates of return should also note that averages of large groups are only a rough indicator for the individual. Even if college graduates experience an average rate of return of 14 percent for the investment in higher education, about one-third of college graduates will do less well financially than the most successful one-third of high school graduates with no college experience.

Another problem inherent in the use of rates of return is that current rates must be estimated on the basis of the earnings record of cohorts educated a number of years before. High school or college graduates of 1970 may conceivably have a rather different earnings experience relative to each other than did their counterparts who entered employment in 1940 or 1950. For example, it seems likely that the last ten years of awareness of civil rights inequities and affirmative action programs will create a lifetime income profile for today's minority student that is different from the profile that his parents' generation is now experiencing. Antidiscrimination policies are likely to be more effective at the margin of new employment of young workers than they are for the average older employee. Thus a generational lag is inherent in such analyses, limiting the usefulness of rate-of-return calculations when applied to current policy choices.

While these methodological issues are important, the basic concept of defining as costs and benefits only those things that can be measured in pecuniary terms is even more problematic. The economic theorist, while not minimizing the problem, would argue for greater efforts to identify the whole array of costs and benefits that do not ordinarily enter into the world of exchange and to devise means of assessing their pecuniary value. Works of art, tickets to the opera, and yoga classes all have reasonably well-established prices, which to a degree reflect the value placed upon them. Even though it is a more difficult task to place precise values on society's gains in the form of literacy, citizenship, social mobility, cohesion, and so on, public policy decisions are, in fact, made in which these benefits are considered by legislators and the executive branch of government.

Such societal benefits, however, do not ordinarily enter into the calculus of the rate of return. The economist tends to be caught up in a quandary not unfamiliar to the philosopher: if one designs a very coarse fish net, does one then only define as *fish* those objects which are caught in the net and do not slip back into the sea? C. F. Carter, a distinguished economist, has argued:

What has gone wrong, both with cost-benefit analysis and with the manpower approach [to public policy concerning higher education], is that we have been led up blind alleys by the economist and have forgotten the real purpose of higher education.... We have damaged the cause of civilization and culture by trying to convince people that they are "good business," and that education has a yield as good as that of a jam factory.... Perhaps the greatest harm which has been done by the jam factory approach is to rob that part of education which is concerned with the summits of human achievement, and with the awe and wonder which surround it.... If the civilization in which we live does not give a high enough importance to the things of the mind, we shall not make things better by pretending that scholarship is the servant of the affluent society (see University of Lancaster, 1972).

Proponents of the cost-benefit calculus are divided between those who tend to minimize the importance of the non-pecuniary benefits of higher education,[1] and those who believe that the net effect of nonpecuniary costs and benefits, could they be measured, would be to substantially *raise* the social rate of return.[2] This latter point of view has apparently been the predominant view of the last several decades, judging by the

---

[1] Milton Friedman has become the most articulate spokesman for this point of view. Although he earlier devoted considerable attention to favorable *neighborhood effects* of education (see "The Role of Government in Education" in his *Capitalism and Freedom,* 1962), he has recently been critical of the consideration of social benefits.

When I first started writing on this subject, I had a good deal of sympathy with this argument. I no longer do. In the interim I have tried time and again to get those who make this argument to be specific about alleged social benefits. Almost always, the answer is simply bad economics.... In my experience, these (social benefits) are always vague and general, and always selective in that negative external effects are never mentioned.... Until this is done, the demand for subsidy in the "public interest" must be regarded as special pleading pure and simple (Friedman, 1968, pp. 110–111).

[2] Howard Bowen has well summarized the view that social benefits are considerable:

Higher education through its instructional activities undoubtedly discovers talent, strengthens leadership in all parts of the economy, makes possible wide applications of high technology, and encourages innovation. Many of these benefits may be appropriated in individual incomes but surely not all of them are.

Higher education raises the quality of civic and business life ... results on the whole in improved home care and training of children ... produces millions of persons who enter essential professions having compensation below rates paid for work requiring less education—for example, teachers, clergymen.... Colleges and universities provide a vast and versatile pool of specialized talent available to society for a wide variety of emergent social problems.... Finally, higher education contributes refinement of conduct, aesthetic appreciation, and taste, and thus adds to the graciousness and variety of life.

Through activities in research, scholarship, criticism, creative art, and public service, higher education also produces social benefits of great value (Bowen & Servelle, 1972, pp. 25–26).

willingness of legislatures to increase the public shares of support for higher education.

One final caveat must be made about the use of rates of return to investment in education in the determination of whether more or less education should be provided. Becker (1964) and others have argued that as long as the yield on such investment is higher than comparable yields for alternative forms of investment it is wise public policy to encourage the provision of more education. While this may be an unassailable point of view, the converse does not necessarily hold—that lower than usual private rates of return imply an overinvestment in education. It is highly likely that a large portion of the contribution of parents and students for college education does not come out of funds that they otherwise would have invested; in fact, it seems more likely that college costs are often borne by reducing or restricting private consumption expenditures. Higher education itself is as much "consumption" as it is "investment" in the minds of many students and parents. Thus, the relevant comparison in judging even the private rate of return may not be what would have been earned on other forms of investment, but rather the willingness of families to forgo or postpone consumption in preference of college education. For many families such a choice might seem to be a rational investment as long as the returns are above zero. And for some families for whom the nonpecuniary advantages of providing their children with a broad education are high, even a negative rate of return would not necessarily be an objection to spending their income on education. One does not need a demonstrable positive rate of return to justify attending a concert or a Shakespeare festival.

In summary, we believe the attempts of economists to determine rates of return on various types and levels of higher education are useful efforts in making intertemporal, and possibly international, comparisons. Quite obviously such efforts would be even more illuminating if all relevant costs and benefits, private and social, could be quantified. We do not believe, however, that such findings are particularly useful in determining whether individuals or societies are underinvesting or overinvesting in higher education. It may be comforting for one to know that he could not have reasonably expected to do as well had he invested his funds in some alternative fashion, but it is not a critical determining factor for most individuals. Students may quite rationally decide to enter one field rather than another on the basis of rough calculations of a similar sort (e.g. "there are good job prospects in health fields, but the future doesn't look as bright in aeronautical engineering"), but to the extent that higher education represents a value judgment on the part of the individual or a society about the kind of life and society one aspires to, no strict pecuniary calculus can do more than suggest hazy guidelines for decision making.

Decisions whether more or less should be invested in higher education will continue to be made by individuals with rationalities that are not susceptible to a strict cost-benefit measurement, and societies will continue to make such decisions through the political forum. Cost-benefit analysis may help us to establish some priorities among forms and levels of education that should receive additional support, although even here there are dangers. If we are less successful in measuring important nonpecuniary benefits than in estimating expected lifetime earnings, then the scales may be tipped too much in favor of education that has clear utilitarian purposes. Cuban higher education in the last ten years, for example, has become almost entirely concentrated on training in agriculture, business, and technical subjects—perhaps a "rational" decision if one does not value, or wish to encourage, independent critical thought and judgment. A second danger of establishing priorities strictly on the basis of rates of return is that many professions have an element of monopoly power by virtue of limited entry or licensing, which may distort private rates of return in a manner than does not truly reflect social yields on investment.

America has long had a genius for providing diverse educational opportunities and for assuring, through a complicated network of subsidies, scholarships, work-study and loan programs, that no highly motivated student of promise is barred from pursuing a collegiate education. We still have some way to go to achieve full equality of educational opportunity, but we believe that the wisest decisions about how much education we, as a society, will avail ourselves of will be made by individuals in their own calculus of advantages and sacrifices. This leaves open the more basic question as to what proportion of costs should be paid directly by the individual and what fraction would be assessed indirectly through taxation—a question to which we turn next.

11. User Benefits versus Societal Benefits

Although the benefits that society derives from having a well-educated populace are difficult to define unambiguously, and even more difficult to quantify, it does not follow that such societal benefits are unimportant. No one would deny the importance in life of love, beauty, and happiness merely because they are impossible to quantify and are perceived somewhat differently by different individuals.

It may be useful to identify several classes of effects of higher education that are not fully reflected by merely summing private economic returns. Some are material in nature, some enhance or weaken the viability of society, and some are principally in the realm of human sensibility.

First, calculations of rates of return provide us with some relative yardsticks of the effects of education on different classes of people, but they may obscure or inadequately reflect real improvements over time in the economic well-being of a society. Advances in knowledge in a society where much basic research is carried on essentially as a public service result in economic gains for society that are not fully reflected in the earnings of those who have produced this new knowledge. Curing disease, splitting the atom, or developing a new hybrid corn may have considerable external economic benefits to society that no university researcher can recapture as a private return.

Similarly, raising the educational level of a society tends to raise the productivity of that society's labor force in a manner that adds to the economic returns of all factors of production—not just to those who have directly benefited from that education. Schultz (1972, p. 11), for example, defines as an *allocative benefit* the ability to discern new opportunities, to evaluate and act on them, and to live comfortably in a world where economic

79

growth constantly creates disequilibria; these are qualities more typical of the educated man, and they contribute to the well-being and progress of society as a whole. Denison (1962) has attempted to identify that portion of long-term economic growth that is attributable to advances in knowledge, and other research by Kendrick (1961), Solow (1957), and others has concluded that a substantial fraction of growth is due to an increase in "total factor productivity" rather than to increasing quantities of labor or capital. Just as the more elementary impacts of the extension of literacy have had a significant economic effect in reducing accidents, enabling the collection of tax revenues, and generally facilitating the process of exchange, so also the qualities of creativity, adaptability, and critical judgment that one often associates with advanced education aid economic growth for society as a whole.

Second, a variety of the effects of higher education are for the most part, although not exclusively, thought to help our society function more effectively. Education enhances the process of socialization; as numerous studies have indicated, the college experience on balance tends to change the attitudes of students in the direction of the dominant norms in American society. Among the more highly educated there is a greater sharing of aesthetic and cultural values, more active political involvement, a greater sense of tolerance toward diverse points of view, a greater openness to economic, social, and political change. These factors contribute to social cohesiveness and tend to reinforce the procedures of a political democracy.

No one who has lived in the academic world for the last 15 years could fail to recognize that the renewal of traditional American values of equality of opportunity, fairness, and non-discrimination have sprung largely from the minds and hearts of college-age youth. The elimination of religious, ethnic, and sex discrimination is closer to reality today in the college-student community than in society at large. Perhaps this single example best illustrates the difficulty of defining (much less measuring) social benefits. For while a large fraction of the citizenry would consider this a significant external benefit of education, some might consider it a social cost. Certainly the civil rights movement in the United States in the 1950s and 1960s was disruptive in many instances, and students have often displayed an intolerance towards their elders, but on balance it seems reasonable to suppose that exercise of critical judgment is beneficial to an open society.

Third, the most elusive category of external effects is that which impinges on the realm of personal values and aspirations for the kind of society one enjoys living in. These might be thought of literally as *neighborhood effects*—the desire of individuals to exist in a world with good neighbors. To the extent that education tends to make one's neighbors more open-minded, alert, physically healthy, liberal in their mind-set (not necessarily in their politics), nonauthoritarian, interested in the community, and more tolerant toward one's own tastes, most people would believe that a well-educated society would be a better society to live in. Most people wish to live in a world of shared (although not necessarily homogenized) values, and would be willing to contribute toward those social institutions and processes that aid in the creation of a friendly society. It is important to most adults not only to obtain a good education for one's own children, but to assure that one's neighbors' children are also educated.

These categories of social benefits are at least suggestive of the types of externalities that are associated with higher education. Among them are some negative as well as positive benefits, but there is considerable historical evidence that American citizens have long thought that on balance these indirect benefits are positive and substantial.

There are a variety of opinions about the optimal pattern of financing higher education, based primarily upon the assumed distribution of personal and societal benefits. At the risk of oversimplification, three positions might be identified that represent the spectrum of opinion.

1   At one extreme are those who believe that the primary benefit of higher education is the enhanced earning power of those who are educated, and that since the *user* reaps the major return on this investment he or she should pay for it. Frequently this point of view will argue for *full-cost pricing* (that is, the elimination of public subsidies to ensure the proper allocation of funds to education) and would meet the equity arguments by assuring the creation of an adequate capital market in the form of guaranteed or income-contingent loans.

2   At the other extreme are those who argue that the societal benefits of higher education are substantial, that anything approaching full-cost pricing would result in a significant underinvestment in higher education (because of the risks and uncertainties facing the student when attempting to make a rational decision at age 18 about the 40 to 50 adult years of his or her life), and that equity is best served by the simplest system to administer—namely, making higher education a free or near-free service to everyone.

3   In between these two points of view is a broad middle ground that might argue that the historical mix of public and private higher education makes a simplistic approach impossible, that the present system has worked reasonably well, and that the present division of the burden of costs is reasonably appropriate in view of the joint private and public benefits that are thought to accrue. Supporters of this position would ordinarily agree that improvements could be made in the present system to ensure the removal of financial obstacles to college attendance, but that it has proved its viability over the years.

Two other points of view cut across these positions, and have not always received the attention they deserve. They focus on the intergenerational sharing of costs and benefits.

One view holds that the financing of education at all levels is essentially an intergenerational transfer—adults fund the education of the young, whether they do so as parents or taxpayers. Pechman has argued that:

There is no way of merging benefits and costs in one distribution to evaluate the equity of the system . . . [apart from forgone earnings] the costs are borne by a generation of people (either parents or taxpayers) who are, in effect, making a gift to those who are going to a public college or university . . . the "fairness" of the method used to finance the costs of public higher education cannot be judged by comparing the taxes and tuition paid by parents with the benefits received by college students. If society decides that higher education should be a public activity, the costs of that activity should be allocated in accordance with the tax system it judges to be best or fairest (Pechman, 1972, pp. 256–257).

The other view is that students "ought" to be emancipated at the time they enter college, and should be encouraged to make rational decisions about their education. Much of the inequity in access to higher education has arisen because it has been assumed that the primary responsibility for paying for college rests on the parent. A fairer system, it can be argued, would make the user generation bear the cost and would recapture the funds advanced for their education through taxes on their later earnings. The chief argument for the income-contingent loan plan is based upon this premise, and some have gone so far as to argue that this should be a compulsory system of funding (as the traditional tax system is) rather than an optional one.[1]

In this sense we might envisage each generation paying for its own education by funding the education of the succeeding generation. To the extent that college education raises one's lifetime earnings it would also raise one's tax contribution in financing the next generation's education. Hartman has attempted to project the effect of this generation's college attendance on their contribution of taxes in later life. Table 24 shows his projections for the distribution of state and local taxes by income group of males age 50 and by college attendance status. He estimates that nearly two-thirds of state and local taxes will be paid by nonusers of the public higher educational system.

[1] Allan Cartter (1972, pp. 189–204) has argued that a portion of the cost (perhaps one-fourth) should be met through a compulsory contingent loan program. However, he argues for an average 50 percent of cost subsidy from tax sources to allow for assumed social benefits.

| | | Nonusers | | |
TABLE 24 Estimated distribution of state and local taxes by income and college attendance status, at age 50 (in percentages) — Income group	Users of public higher education	No college	Private college	Total
Under $3,000	0.5%	1.0%	0.2%	1.7%
$3,000–$6,000	2.2	5.9	0.7	8.8
$6,000–$10,000	9.0	20.3	3.0	32.3
$10,000–$15,000	10.9	12.5	4.3	27.7
Over $15,000	14.7	7.2	7.6	29.5
Total taxes	37.3%	46.9%	15.8%	100.0%

SOURCE: Computed from data in Hartman (1972*a*, p. 160).

Table 25 compares the three education groups by giving the estimated distributions of male income earners at age 50, of their shares of total income received by the age cohort, and of their shares of state and local and federal income taxes.

State and local taxes have a moderately regressive impact; nonattenders are estimated to receive 44.9 percent of the total income of the cohort but pay 46.9 percent of these taxes. By contrast, the federal income tax has a progressive impact, and nonattenders pay only 37.5 percent. If we assume that the income effects in later life were entirely due to the college experience (a heroic assumption that is obviously only partly true) then we could say that the representative student who attends a tax-supported public institution will receive an income 15 percent higher than the average male at age 50, and that the representative nonattender will have an income 16 percent below the average income for all males. State and local tax payments, however, are only 12 percent above average for the user and 9 percent lower than average for the nonattender.

Under present income patterns and state and local tax rates, this means that the public college attender, at age 50, would receive an income approximately $4,500 larger than the noncollege attender, and would pay about $210 more in annual state and local taxes. (The private college alumnus is anticipated to have an income 27 percent above the nonattender, and tax payments 21 percent above average). Thus, although the public college attender, by virtue of his expected larger income later in life, will pay more in state and local taxes, the increment will make only a modest contribution toward the subsidy of his education.

By contrast, under our reasonably progressive federal income

	Users of public higher education	Nonusers		Total
		No college	*Private college*	
Males in age cohort	33.4%	53.6%	13.0%	100.0%
Income received	38.5	44.9	16.6	100.0
State and local taxes	37.3	46.9	15.8	100.0
Federal income tax	39.2	37.5	23.3	100.0

TABLE 25 *Estimated distribution of males aged 50 years, shares of total income, and shares of state and local and federal income taxes, by college attendance status (in percentages)*

SOURCE: Computed from data in Hartman (1972*a*, p. 161).

tax structure, the typical public college attender, at age 50, is likely to pay about $1,500 annually in additional federal taxes. One of the strongest reasons, therefore, for a larger proportion of the public support of higher education to come from federal, rather than state and local, tax sources is that the federal treasury captures a larger share of the income advantage that results from higher personal earnings on the part of college graduates.

The Commission has been critical of the regressive tax structures in many states because a high proportion of the costs of public higher education are paid for by those who receive no direct benefit. In *The Capitol and the Campus* (1971a) we urged states to develop more progressive tax systems in the interests of greater equity and adequacy in the financing of education and other social services. Heavier reliance on progressive state income taxes would provide both a more adequate revenue base for state programs, and assure that the income advantages of college attendance would accrue more to the state governments, which traditionally bear the largest share of the cost of providing higher education.

Considerable interest has been shown in recent years in income-contingent loan plans, chiefly because they are a form of "user tax" and would place more of the financial burden of paying for higher education on those who directly benefit from it. Under the Educational Opportunity Bank Plan proposed by the Zacharias committee in 1967, students could pay back loans entirely upon the basis of income received after graduation. Thus it would approximate a special tax applicable only to educational users, with exemptions provided for low earners (Panel on Educational Innovation, 1967).

If it were clear that all of the benefits of higher education accrued to the student, then some form of user tax would be a reasonable way of paying for higher education. College tuition, paid currently, is one such form of user tax; the advantage of deferred plans, such as income-contingent repayment plans, is that the student is not confronted by a financial obstacle at the time of going to college, and shares the repayment risks with many others over a lifetime of earnings.

At the other extreme, if one assumes that the primary benefits of higher education accrue to society in general rather than to the individual, then a progressive income tax might be deemed the most equitable means of paying for higher education.

In fact, the benefits are neither all personal nor all societal, but some blend of the two, which supports the viewpoint that a mixed system of individual and governmental financing of higher education is appropriate. To the extent that the education and training of students is the essential purpose of colleges and universities, however, it would appear that the social benefits of education are similar in nature and extent whether a student attends a public or a private college or university. Yet, when we view the aggregate accounts, the educational funds of institutions derived from tax revenues are nearly 80 percent in public institutions, and only 15 percent in the private colleges and universities (Table 4). Conversely, students and their families pay about 60 percent of the educational costs in tuition fees in private institutions, and only 17 percent of the costs in public institutions.

State-supported colleges, and to a less extent private colleges, serve other societal functions in addition to the education of young persons—through extension services, continuing education, research, cultural activities, and community service. The Commission has urged that greater attention be given by the states to the needs of the private colleges and universities—preferably through expanded student assistance, but possibly by direct aid as in New York—for these institutions serve many of the same public purposes and add to both the strength and diversity of educational offerings available to a state's citizens.

Quite apart from the question of whether the benefits of higher education are essentially personal or shared by society as a whole, renewed interest has been shown in recent years in the question of user charges for several quite practical reasons. One is that the governmental costs of higher education have soared as the percentage of the age group attending college has risen. In a state such as New York, for example, state support of higher education has climbed from $100 million in 1960 to over $1 billion in 1972. A second reason is that it has become increasingly apparent that the private colleges and universities are unlikely to retain their vitality in the years immediately ahead if the tuition differential between public and private institutions continues to widen. A healthy mixed system of higher education is more likely to be maintained with a diminished tuition gap and additional direct aid to students—a direction taken by the federal government under the Higher Education Act of 1972. But perhaps more importantly, the rising pressure for student "emancipation," encouraged by the lowering of the voting age and mandated in some states by making age 18 the legal age of majority, has renewed interest in devising ways in which the student can take greater responsibility for his or her education. The possible disappearance of out-of-state fee structures in public institutions, if courts rule that a student's legal domicile is his college residence, is one more pressure in the direction of treating the 18-year-old as an economically independent adult. It seems possible that the traditional assumption of primary parental responsibility for financing the private costs of higher education will be eroded over the next decade or two, and that new means will be devised to provide the individual student with access to funds for his or her education.

In Sweden today the university student assumes these burdens for himself at age 20, but has the power of drawing against future pension rights in borrowing to meet the costs of further education. In a recent conference, Gösta Rehn, director for Manpower and Social Affairs of the Organisation for Economic Co-operation and Development (Paris), has proposed for OECD-member countries that higher education, paid educational leaves during one's working lifetime, and retirement all be seen as part of a work-study-leisure continuum and be funded centrally through a social insurance mechanism (Rehn, 1972).

The Carnegie Commission, in *Less Time, More Options* (1971b), proposed that "all persons, after high school graduation have two years of postsecondary education placed 'in the bank' for them to be withdrawn at any time in their lives when it best suits them." As one looks toward the 1980s, it seems increasingly likely that beyond the first two years of college, user charges will become a more substantial source of support for higher education. In fact, we believe that after the first two years of college, the emphasis in student-aid programs should gradually shift toward deferred payment or contingent loan plans. Several leading universities are experimenting with such plans, and there have been proposals for such plans at the state level. It also seems probable that greater public recognition will be given to the fact that societal benefits are similar in nature and magnitude, if not identical, from private or public colleges and universities.

The Commission concludes that although the portion of total educational costs borne by the average student and parent should remain approximately what it is today, a gradual redistribution of this burden in a manner that will ensure greater equity within the system will be necessary.

12. The Level and Quality of Education

In general discussions of higher education there is a tendency to treat college education as though it were an undifferentiated whole. Obviously it is not. Most public systems are divided among community colleges, four-year colleges, and state universities. And there are significant qualitative differences within and among states in both their private and public sectors. Students are not randomly distributed among institutions, so attention must be paid to the sorting process in considerations of equity.

The California system of higher education is perhaps the clearest and oldest example of a differentiated system. Students must be in the top 12½ percent of their high school class to be eligible for entry to any of the University of California campuses as a freshman, and in the top one-third for entry into one of the four-year state colleges (now renamed in most cases the California State University). All high school graduates are eligible to attend any of the public community colleges in the state. Thus admission to senior institutions is based upon student performance.[1]

Table 26 shows the estimated distribution of parental income of undergraduates in the four educational sectors in 1971–72, according to an approximate 25 percent sample of students surveyed by the California State Scholarship and Loan Commis-

---

[1] Transfer from one tier to another is somewhat freer than the freshman entrance standards might suggest, and depends upon performance in the initial institution. In spring 1972, approximately 17 percent of University of California students were transfers from community colleges, and nearly 9 percent were transfers from other four-year institutions. In the California State University and Colleges system the corresponding percentages were 45 percent and 9 percent (California State Scholarship and Loan Commission, 1972, p. 204).

TABLE 26   *Income of parents of students attending four categories of California institutions, 1971-72*

Family income group	University of California	California State University	Community colleges	Private colleges	All
Under $3,000	7.3%	11.1%	12.1%	7.4%	9.5%
$3,000–$6,000	8.0	9.9	13.1	7.0	9.6
$6,000–$9,000	11.8	16.1	19.0	12.0	14.7
$9,000–$12,000	13.4	17.8	16.0	13.9	15.2
$12,000–$15,000	13.7	15.3	14.2	14.0	14.3
$15,000–$21,000	19.7	16.8	14.1	18.4	17.5
Over $21,000	26.2	13.2	11.5	27.3	19.2
TOTAL	100.1	100.2	100.0	100.0	100.0
Mean family income	$15,160	$12,330	$11,420	$15,650	$12,820

SOURCE: California State Scholarship and Loan Commission (1972, p. 193).

sion. The distributions of the private sector and the University of California were almost identical, while the four-year colleges and community colleges drew more heavily from less affluent families.

In a study of the public higher educational system in California several years ago, Hansen and Weisbrod (1969) attempted to identify the beneficiaries of taxpayer subsidies. For 1965 they determined that the average annual state subsidy per student was approximately $720 in the community colleges, $1,400 in the state colleges, and $1,700 in the University of California. Comparing these subsidies with estimated state and local taxes paid by the average parent of a college student, they concluded that the net transfer (subsidy less taxes paid) was $40 for families with children attending the community colleges, and $630 and $790 respectively for the state college and university sectors.

In a lively response, Joseph Pechman (1970) recalculated tax burdens and subsidies by income class, including families who did not have children in college, and concluded that the lowest class (below $2,000) was a net gainer, while those above paid more in taxes than was received in educational subsidies.

These two seemingly contradictory conclusions are not necessarily inconsistent with one another, and they accentuate the problem of assessing the equity of any pattern of financing. What is clear is that local taxes, which in many states are a substantial source of funding for community colleges, are usually more regressive than state tax structures. Moreover, community colleges tend to serve a student audience drawn more heavily from low-income families who face proportionately high combined state and local tax rates. At the other extreme, the more heavily subsidized university sector of the higher education system tends to serve students with considerably higher average family incomes, and these families in most states have a proportionately lower state and local tax burden.

Table 27 shows the percentage of the 18 to 24 age cohort who were enrolled as undergraduates in public and private colleges in October 1971, according to United States census data. Low-income families begin with the handicap that a smaller percentage graduate from high school. Somewhat surprisingly, only one-fourth of students from families with incomes under $7,500 attended public community colleges. Middle- and upper-income groups (above $10,000) are two to three times as likely to attend college as those in lower-income groups. Interestingly, even in the highest-income category, over 70 percent of enrolled undergraduates were in public, rather than private, colleges. At the low end of the income scale (below $5,000) the private colleges enroll 18.7 percent of undergraduates, as contrasted with only 15.1 percent in the $5,000–$10,000 range and 23.8 percent from families with incomes over $10,000.[2]

To the extent students are sorted out between two-year and four-year colleges on the basis of real ability, or to the extent the presence of a community college enables a capable student to attend college who might otherwise have been unable to do so for other than strictly financial reasons, the lower subsidy per student in the two-year college section should not be a matter of major concern. This low subsidy is a means of conserving scarce resources to maximize the educational benefit to society. The alternative of lottery admission to two- and four-year college and

[2] A study of New York high school graduates in 1970 showed that 11.1 percent enrolling in the tuition-free City University were from families with $5,000 or less income, while 13.3 percent enrolling in the 23 private colleges and universities in New York City were from that income group. At the other end of the income scale 10.9 percent at CUNY and 13.3 percent at private four-year colleges had family incomes above $15,000. Thus, while the public institutions minimize the financial obstacle to admission to college by low tuition and fees, it would be an error to conclude that public institutions primarily serve the lower- and middle-income groups while private institutions serve the affluent (City University of New York, 1971).

TABLE 27 Percentage of 18- to 24-year age population currently enrolled as undergraduates in public and private colleges, by family income level, fall 1971

	Public institutions			Private institutions			Total
Family income	*2-year*	*4-year*	*Total public*	*2-year*	*4-year*	*Total private*	*attending college*
Under $3,000	2.2%	7.8%	10.0%	0.4%	1.9%	2.3%	12.3%
$3,000–$5,000	3.1	8.8	−1.9	0.3	2.4	2.7	14.6
$5,000–$7,500	4.4	8.0	12.4	0.2	1.8	2.1	14.5
$7,500–$10,000	5.2	10.3	15.4	0.2	2.7	2.9	18.3
$10,000–$15,000	7.5	14.6	22.1	0.4	5.1	5.5	27.6
Over $15,000	8.6	24.8	33.3	0.8	11.6	12.4	45.7
All income groups	5.6	12.8	18.3	0.4	4.4	4.8	23.1

SOURCE: Computed from U.S. Bureau of the Census, *Current Population Reports,* ser. P-20, no. 236, (1972, Table 8) and no. 241 (1972, Table 14).

university campuses might appear on the surface to be more equitable in strictly financial terms but it would be a very inefficient way to conduct the education function.

Every attempt should be made to ensure that two-year colleges, particularly in dense urban locations, do not become educational ghettos for low-income families who cannot afford to send their children to senior colleges. Adequate financial aid should be available to assist the bright student to attend the college that best fits his capabilities. The Commission also has strongly urged policies that would make it easier for the community-college student to transfer to senior college for his upper-division years based upon his performance in the first two years. We believe that differentiation by ability, with open doors to higher-level study, will effectively serve both equity and efficiency goals.

13. *Graduate and Advanced Professional Education*

The financing of graduate-level education differs from that of undergraduate education in a number of important respects: It is commonly much more costly to the institutions, particularly at the doctoral level; students are older and can no longer expect the same degree of parental support, and since World War II, federal agencies have played a key role in the direct support of students, training programs, and related research activities.

Two different philosophies have been evident in the support of students at the postbaccalaureate level over the last two decades. Advanced professional students in such fields as law, medicine, and dentistry have been predominantly self-supporting; until the last several years, fellowship funds have been relatively scarce, chiefly on the argument that the private returns to investment in professional education are high and that therefore students could be expected to borrow against future earnings. By contrast, in the arts and sciences a high proportion (50 percent or more) of doctoral students have been traditionally supported by federal, foundation, or institutional fellowship funds, or appointments to teaching or research assistantships. This support has developed largely because societal returns have appeared to be significantly high and private returns relatively low in the academic disciplines.

Over the last several years, as manpower shortages in health-related fields became more evident and as the shortage of Ph.D. scientists appeared to abate, there was a reversal in these trends in external support. Federal fellowship support for Ph.D. students peaked in 1969, and has dropped sharply over the last several years. Concurrently support for students in health-related fields climbed until 1973, although the 1973–74 federal budget calls for a reduction in such student aid. In all fields, need has become an increasingly important criterion for support, and much greater emphasis is placed today upon increasing the representation of women and ethnic minorities in the professions.

Table 28 shows the amount of federal support going to graduate students in 1969 and 1972, with federal estimates for 1973 and 1974 based on 1973–74 budgét reports. The phasing out of NASA and NDEA fellowships and the sharp decline in NSF fellowship and traineeship programs have been partially offset over the last five years by the increase in the enrollment of veterans under the GI Bill, but beginning in 1974 it is anticipated that the number of eligible veterans will also decrease. The 1973–74 budget also introduces a curtailment of NIH funds for students in health-related fields. Thus, the prospect for direct federal aid to graduate students is now rather gloomy in all areas.

Data on the support of graduate students are poor, but a rough picture of the current situation in the arts and sciences—which represent about 55 percent of advanced degree enrollments—can be pieced together. Table 29 attempts this for 1972–73.

Based upon the Council of Graduate Schools fall 1972 enrollment survey, there were approximately 285,000 full-time graduate students in the arts and sciences in 1972–73, plus about 310,000 part-time students, or an FTE total of about 400,000. Nearly three-fourths of graduate students appear to receive assistance from some source other than family resources, al-

TABLE 28 *Federal outlays in support of graduate students, 1969, 1972, and budget estimates for 1973 and 1974 (in millions of dollars)*

Agency	1969 actual	1972 actual	1973 estimate	1974 estimate
H.E.W.				
N.I.H.	$182	$207	$254	$168
Office of Education	41	49	57	41
Other	16	70	66	51
Veterans Administration	161	190	245	227
National Science Foundation	48	30	20	14
NASA, Justice, etc.	15	15	16	7
	$463	$561	$658	$508

SOURCE: The Federal Budget.

	Form or source of assistance	Number of students (in thousands)	Amount of assistance (in millions of dollars)
1.	Research assistantships	45	$135
2.	Other service assistantships	65	160
3.	Fellowships, reported by institutions	40	80
4.	Office of Education	165	57
5.	Other federal assistance	40	102
6.	Veterans receiving benefits	103	147
		458	$681
	Less allowance for double counting	−160	
		298	

TABLE 29 Graduate students assistance: estimates for 1972–73

SOURCES OF ESTIMATES: Lines 1 and 2: The Fall 1972 Council of Graduate Schools survey of graduate schools, which reported information for institutions enrolling about 90 percent of graduate students in the arts and sciences, reported 109,027 assistantships requiring services. The division between research and teaching assistantships (RA's and TA's) has been estimated based on a report for the early 1960s (Walters, 1965, Table 12). Amounts have been estimated assuming $2,500 per TA and $3,000 per RA.

Line 3: The CGS survey reported 47,270 fellowships held by graduate students. This number has been increased by 10 percent to allow for incomplete response to the survey, and reduced to eliminate double counting with federal fellowships in lines 4 and 5. Average amounts are estimated at $2,000.

Lines 4 and 5: As reported by the Federal Bureau of the Budget.

Line 6: 60 percent of figure reported by the Bureau of the Budget. Approximately 40 percent of advanced degree enrollment was in professional fields outside the arts and sciences.

though it should be noted that the assistantship positions require services and are not grants-in-aid, and that a significant part of the number reported by the Office of Education are likely to be borrowers who receive only an interest subsidy. Nonetheless, the total amount of assistance is considerably larger than the total tuition and fee charges to graduate students in the arts and sciences, indicating that the financing of graduate education is quite unlike the common pattern at the undergraduate level.

We can conclude that either through external funding, where governmental or institutional agencies have determined that the societal benefits of encouraging graduate study were large, or through the creation of study-related work opportunities within the academic institution, graduate level tuition charges in the arts and sciences are seldom paid by the student unaided. It would make only a minor difference if tuition charges at this level were higher or lower; the public-private distribution of costs is likely to remain about the same. There may be good institutional reasons to set graduate tuition charges by the same standards used in determining tuition at undergraduate and professional levels, but consequent adjustments in fellowship and assistantship levels are likely to minimize any impact upon the relative contribution by private individuals and public subsidies.

Graduate students, partly because they are older and more likely to be financially independent of their parents, and partly because of the availability of financial assistance, more customarily choose their graduate school in a national—rather than a strictly local or regional—context. This is especially true of Ph.D. candidates. Out-of-state fees in most public universities are reasonably competitive with tuitions charged by private universities, and even in-state fees are sometimes higher than for prebaccalaureate education. Thus there is not the wide difference in nominal or real (net of student aid) tuition levels that exists for undergraduates. The Commission therefore sees less cause for concern regarding relative tuition charges of public and private institutions at this level of study than it does in the case of the undergraduate level. There is, also, less cause for concern about differential opportunities for students from lower- and higher-income families.

In the fields of advanced professional study, where personal returns to education have been significantly greater than for most graduate study, borrowing is a more common and effective pattern of financing. In recent years grant-in-aid funds have increased to assist the needy student and to encourage a greater representation of ethnic minorities, but self-financing is likely to remain the predominant pattern. Because of the high cost of education in many of the health fields, federal policy has been directed more toward supporting institutions and thus subsidizing the tuition level. Because the major obstacle to adjusting the manpower flows to rising demand levels in such fields is the limited capacity of institutions rather than a shortage of capable students, federal policy has been more directed to encouraging institutional expansion.

There is a considerable potential public benefit from providing incentives for students to enter highly skilled and professional public service occupations that have long-term manpower shortages. Science and engineering fields, and the academic professions in general, benefited from greatly increased federal funding in the post-Sputnik period. Today, however, because many fields are developing manpower surpluses, and because the need for additional college teachers seems likely to decline as we move toward enrollment stabilization, the societal benefit of continuing high subsidies is also declining. Thus, federal policy is now one of constraint. The 1973–74 budget reflects the same view toward future needs in the health fields, because federal assistance for both students and institutions is scheduled to decline for the first time in many years. Too great a reliance on manpower assessments in determining public funding, however, tends to overlook the delicate balance of institutional well-being; what may appear to be a rational policy in adjusting manpower flows may exact a harsh penalty on the institutions whose continued vitality is essential to the public interest. The Commission urges that the effective long-term stability of universities, which perform valuable services as national laboratories for research and renewal, should be an important element in the public policy calculus.

14. Policy Considerations and Recommendations

POLICY CONSID-
ERATIONS Over the course of the present century the public (taxpayer) share of college costs has been rising. This increase is largely due to the growing proportion of students in low-tuition public institutions, and particularly to the expanding community college sector since World War II. As a steadily rising proportion of the nation's youth completes high school and chooses to go to college, the public cost of higher education grows much more rapidly than the national income.

The Commission believes that access to higher education should be expanded so that, within the total system of higher education in each state, every high school graduate or otherwise qualified person will have an opportunity to pursue postsecondary studies. This does not mean that every young person should of necessity attend college—many will choose not to attend, and others will not benefit sufficiently from attendance to justify their time and the expense involved. Thus, as we have previously set forth in *A Chance to Learn* (1970*a*) and in *The Open-Door Colleges* (1970*b*), we favor universal access but not universal attendance.

If the proportion of youth going to college continues to rise, and if most of the additional students are from families that cannot afford to make a significant contribution to the costs of college attendance, even greater public resources must be devoted to higher education over the next 10 to 15 years. This raises the question of whether traditional forms and levels of support from both public and private sources will be adequate to the task.

The policy of low tuition or no tuition in public higher education appealed strongly to the founders of state-supported institutions and their respective legislatures in the nineteenth century. With populations that were predominantly agricultural,

99

and containing relatively few wealthy families and far fewer members of the middle class than is true today, a policy of low tuition seemed the most logical way of providing an opportunity for participation in higher education to the relatively small number of sons and daughters of farmers and shopkeepers who completed secondary school. It was argued that a policy of heavily subsidized public higher education would contribute to the economic growth and development of the state or region by providing a supply of educated young people who would become the doctors, lawyers, teachers, and business leaders needed in a developing society. And, as industrialization proceeded, the need for adequate numbers of engineers, scientists, and technicians was equally evident.

Today these arguments are beginning to be seriously challenged in a number of states. The Board of Regents of the University of California voted to abandon its historic policy of no tuition in 1970,[1] and tuition levels in many other state colleges and universities (particularly for out-of-state students) have risen significantly in the last year or two. This apparent change in the historical policy is partly a reflection of the emergence of other pressing social service needs that are now successfully competing for public revenues (e.g., in health, welfare, and environmental areas), but it is also a natural consequence of the cost of rapid expansion of educational opportunities to a majority of youth. In addition, the traditional pride that voters took in "our state university" may have been somewhat dissipated by the growth of complex multi-institution or multi-campus systems of public higher education, and was tarnished by several years of student dissent and violence on campuses.

In recent years the literature of criticism of traditional funding patterns has also been growing. Supporters of the viewpoint that the prime benefit of higher education is personal and pecuniary have argued for full-cost pricing—or sometimes merely full-instructional-salary-cost pricing—and the improvement of capital markets to serve the student population. Others have argued that low (or zero) tuition policies disproportionately favor upper- and middle-income families, and in some cases actually redistribute income from the poor to the relatively affluent.

---

[1] For 1973–74, tuition and fee charges average $640 for resident and $2,400 for out-of-state undergraduate students at the university campuses.

The Commission believes, however, that existing patterns of tuition charges should be modified only gradually, and that the overall proportion of economic costs met by students and their families should not be substantially increased. Indeed, it may be necessary to decrease the proportion temporarily as more students from low-income families are accommodated in the 1970s. But we believe that it is unrealistic to ask public bodies—and, ultimately, the taxpayers—to add the full incremental funding in the coming decade sufficient to meet an increase in enrollment of perhaps 30 to 40 percent, plus an approximate 30 percent increase in per student costs over the general inflation rate even under conservative assumptions (in accordance with the Commission's recommendations in *The More Effective Use of Resources*). Thus, we believe that greater attention must be devoted to the pricing structure of higher education and that it may have to be modified to assure the adequacy of funds for normal expansion, greater equalization of opportunity, and the maintenance of effective educational quality.

Public subsidies for higher education can be defended by the existence of societal benefits—although individuals differ in their estimation of the magnitude of those benefits. It should be noted, however, that the fact that external benefits accrue to society in general is not sufficient justification for a general subsidy; it also needs to be demonstrated that private decisions and initiative would not produce that same social benefit. It seems clear to us that private decisions under the existing array of options open to students do not produce the same result that society at large would select today; but it also seems clear that taxpayer subsidies are not now allocated to maximize societal benefits. A significant proportion of students who attend college would do so in any event, with or without the subsidy provided to all students in tax-supported institutions, and a significant proportion who do not now attend would do so if existing financial obstacles were removed.[2]

---

[2] In a recent study Peltzman (1973) estimates that over one-half of public subsidies to higher education—and perhaps as much as three-fourths—displace private funds that would have been spent for the same purpose in the absence of subsidies. Peltzman makes a case that a subsidy-in-kind (in the form of low tuition) is much less effective than an equivalent money subsidy, and under some circumstances may actually reduce the total amount of educational services used by the public. He concludes that social efficiency considerations argue for targeted direct subsidies to students in need.

Several new conditions are present today that indicate a significant change in the environment in which higher education will live in the coming decade or two, and we believe that these changing conditions call for a reassessment of traditional views about the financing of higher education. These new circumstances are:

The approach of enrollment conditions more akin to a stationary state than to the constant pattern of growth we have been accustomed to

The rapid widening of the tuition differential between public and private institutions in the period 1950 to 1970

The emerging financial difficulties of many private institutions

The growth of competing social claims upon public resources

The new philosophy of federal support of higher education, which features direct aid to students, and which, in the Higher Education Act of 1972, accepts as a federal responsibility basic funding of educational opportunities for youth from low-income families

These factors lead us to conclude that changes in the future funding pattern of higher education should be made in such a way as to make the distribution of public support more selective—targeted to help those most in need of financial aid. We do not favor abrupt change; rather, we believe that a gradual shift in pricing policy and public support programs should be undertaken over the next decade with three major goals:

1 to minimize the financial obstacle to college attendance, and thus to implement the principle of universal access to college education

2 to seek to improve equity in the funding pattern of higher education, both in direct charges to students and parents, and in indirect charges to the taxpayers in general

3 to retain and strengthen the vitality of the diverse system of public and private institutions of higher education

It would be a major error of public policy to implement universal access with primary reliance upon a regressive tax structure, to strengthen private institutions merely by raising tuition levels in public institutions, or to assume that equity considerations involve only the tuition and scholarship policies of public colleges. All three of the enumerated goals must be kept in the forefront in any wise selection of public policy.

In 1970–71 the distribution of total costs of higher education by income source was as follows:

	Family	Taxpayers	Philanthropy	Total
Total monetary outlays on higher education	37%	54%	9%	100%
Total economic costs (including forgone earnings)	64	31	5	100

We believe that the first priority in higher education today is to move as rapidly as possible toward the equalization of opportunity to attend college. The achievement of universal access, in the first instance, will require some shift in the share of direct costs borne by the family to the taxpayers as more low-income students enter higher education dependent more on public aid and less on parental support. Such a shift is envisaged in the Higher Education Act of 1972, with the implementation of the Basic Opportunity Grants program, and has been recommended in earlier reports of the Carnegie Commission. As this shift develops, we see the pattern becoming approximately the following by the early 1980s:

	Family	Taxpayer	Philanthropy	Total
Total monetary outlays on higher education	34%	58%	8%	100%
Total economic costs (including forgone earnings)	65	32	5	100*

*Total does not add to 100 because of rounding
SOURCE: Appendix E.

In the longer run, however, particularly as family incomes keep rising and as college attendance becomes more widespread at all income levels, we anticipate that somewhat greater reliance will again be placed upon personal resources and somewhat less reliance on governmental sources, which will tend to restore the current balance. In this process, however, we should expect that the burden among families would gradually be redistributed in accordance with ability to pay within both the public and private sectors of higher education.

We conclude that the overall division of economic costs that has evolved historically between families, taxpayers, and philanthropy should not be greatly altered.

SHARING THE COST BURDEN

Recommendation 1: <u>Over the next few years, the taxpayer share of monetary outlays in higher education should be increased modestly, as student-aid funds expand to assist students from low-income families.</u>

But then we anticipate that the family share will increase gradually again as disposable incomes and ability to pay improve.

The approximate one-third direct monetary outlay burden shouldered by the student and family, two-thirds by taxpayer subsidies and philanthropic gifts (these relative contributions are reversed when total economic costs including forgone income are viewed) seems to us to be a reasonable and justifiable pattern of support for higher education. Within this pattern, however, we believe that significant progress could be made toward the goals presented above by a gradual redistribution of the burden within the family and taxpayer categories.

In the case of taxpayer support it is clear that the primary reliance upon state tax revenues for the subsidy of higher education places an undue burden on the lower-income groups in many states. As Table 12 indicated, the burden of state and local taxes is considerably higher as a percentage of income for low-income families than for those in middle- and upper-income groups.[3]

Federal tax revenues are derived largely from personal and corporate income taxes and are not only more equitable, but revenues also tend to rise about 40 percent more rapidly than personal income. The chief reason is that, as personal income

[3] Table 12 showed effective rates of 10.7 percent for the under-$3,000 group declining to 7.0 percent for the over-$10,000 group, estimated from tax payments deductible for federal income tax payments. The President's Council of Economic Advisers estimated the incidence of state and local taxes as ranging from 11 percent for the $2,000–$4,000 group to 7 percent for over $15,000 for 1965. Below $2,000 the estimate was 26 percent of income, but transfer payments to that group were larger than tax payments by the group. (See *Economic Report of the President*, 1969, p. 161).

rises, families tend to move into higher tax brackets. The revenue from state and local taxes, by contrast, tends to rise less rapidly than personal income. As a result, state and local governments find that they must raise tax *rates* to meet rising costs, and, with regressive tax structures, higher tax rates mean disproportionately increased tax burdens for those with low income.

Recommendation 2: <u>States with regressive tax structures should develop more progressive tax systems in the interest of greater equity and adequacy in the financing of education and other public services.</u>

In light of the greater responsiveness of federal tax revenues to the gradual rise of income levels, due to the progressivity of federal taxes, it seems sensible to expect the federal share of the direct support of higher education to increase over the coming decade. About 36 percent of the public support for higher education (excluding three-fourths of contract research, which is considered to be mostly a purchase of services, but including veterans' educational benefits), now comes from federal sources (Table 30). Federal funds can more effectively provide for greater regional equality in the provision of educational opportunities, and federal programs are already playing a significant role in lowering the financial barriers to college attendance among the less well-to-do. If all federal expenditures for contract research are included, the federal share amounts to about 45 percent.

When fully funded, the Higher Education Act of 1972, with its $1,400 Basic Opportunity Grants, will be a major step toward implementing the policies that have been recommended by the Commission.

Recommendation 3: <u>The balance of public support for higher education must shift over the coming decade if the goal of universal access is to be achieved, and federal funds should partially relieve the states of added financial burdens resulting from the expected expansion in higher education. We recommend that federal support of higher education should gradually expand to about one-half of the total governmental contributions by the early 1980s.</u>

Federal government

  Institutional support

    Research — $ 615   (2,460)*

    Other† — 1,330

  Assistance to students

    Veterans' benefits — 1,117

    Other† — 930

  Total federal — $ 3,992   (5,837)*

State and local government

  Institutional support — $ 7,604

  Student assistance — 336

  Total state and local — $ 7,940

  Combined total, all government — $11,932   (13,777)*

  Federal share of governmental support — 33.5%   (42.4%)*

  Federal contribution, as percentage of total educational funds of institutions — 24.9%

  Federal contribution, as percentage of total institutional funds — (23.7%)*

SOURCE: Computed from Tables 3, 4, and Appendix A, Table A-14.

*Figures in parentheses include all federal sponsored research; other figures include one-fourth of research funds as support of education (see Appendix B).

† Some funds which support institutional programs are in turn used to aid students; thus a precise distinction cannot be made between these two categories of support. Of the $575 million reported by institutions as "Student aid income from public sources," $475 million has been assumed to come from the federal government and $100 million from states apart from general state scholarship programs. The remaining federal expenditures under student assistance are principally social security dependents' benefits.

The federal contribution, as we envisage it, will consist primarily of direct aid to students, increased support of graduate education, including training in public service professions, and the support of research activities. In 1970–71 about 65 percent of all student-assistance-grant funds came through federal sources (including veterans' and Old Age Survivors and Disability and Health Insurance (OASDHI) dependents' benefits); we anticipate by the early 1980s that about three-fourths of a larger aid figure will come from federal support.[4] Similarly, although the 1973–74 federal budget is not cause for great op-

---

[4] Federal and state grants to students are likely to be much larger than in 1970–71, but, assuming continued peace, veterans' benefits are likely to be minimal by then.

timism in the short-run, we believe that over the coming decade the federal government must significantly increase its support of education in graduate and selected professional fields and of basic research if the nation is to remain in the vanguard of scientific and technological developments. Each of these is an area of clear national responsibility and cannot effectively be left to state and institutional action alone.

Just as we recommend a shift in the balance of public support for higher education, so we also believe that gradual adjustments will be needed in institutional tuition policy. The Commission believes that there is a case for restructuring the tuition policies of public institutions of higher education, so that tuition would be comparatively low for lower-division students, somewhat higher for upper-division students, and considerably higher for graduate students, for the following reasons:

1 Lower-division students, especially at relatively open access institutions, such as community colleges, are often uncertain about their prospects for academic achievement in college, and thus may be especially reluctant to finance their education through borrowing.

2 A low-tuition policy for lower-division students, especially for students in community colleges, would help to implement the Commission's policy of universal access to higher education, as set forth in *A Chance to Learn* and in *The Open-Door Colleges.*

3 The cost of education per student is relatively low at the lower-division level, rises somewhat at the upper-division level, and is relatively high for graduate education. Thus, with uniform tuition at all three levels, the lower-division student pays a disproportionately high percentage of his costs of education. Studies conducted at the University of Toronto and information obtained from a number of public institutions in the United States indicate that the cost of education per student at the upper-division level is commonly about 50 percent higher (and more at some institutions) than at the lower-division level, and that the cost of education for graduate students is two to three or even more times as high as the average cost for undergraduates. Adjusting tuition in four-year institutions more equitably to costs of education would bring lower-division charges to students closer to those at public community colleges and en-

able low-income students to choose more freely among public institutions for lower-division instruction.

4 The earning capacity of students rises with increasing education, so that, as students move into upper-division and graduate levels, they are more able to earn at least part of their educational costs through part-time work, summer jobs, or stopping out for a year or two. They also should be less reluctant to borrow funds.

In earlier reports of the Commission (e.g., *The Capitol and the Campus*, 1971a) we advocated "a policy of free or nominal tuition for the first two years," particularly for short-term technical and vocational education programs. We reiterate our belief that educational opportunities should be available in the community colleges *at little or no net cost to the student*. However, the enactment of the Higher Education Act of 1972, when it receives adequate funding, should assure even the most economically disadvantaged student of the means to contribute up to 50 percent to the cost of his or her education. Thus, although the Commission reaffirms its belief that the first two years of college in public institutions—and most particularly in the community colleges—should be essentially without cost for the student with no adequate means of financing his or her education, it recognizes that this condition may appropriately be achieved by a policy that combines low tuition charges and generous grants-in-aid to students of limited means.

TUITION POLICY   Recommendation 4: Public institutions—and especially the community colleges—should maintain a relatively low-tuition policy for the first two years of higher education. Such tuition should be sufficiently low that no student, after receipt of whatever federal and state support he or she may be eligible for, is barred from access to some public institution by virtue of inadequate finances.

"Relatively low tuition," in this context, means at such a level that, after the receipt of basic federal student-aid grants and whatever state aid a student may be eligible for, the student from a very low-income family would find the net outlay required to attend college for the first two years approximately zero. Beyond the first two years, however, we believe that a student (or his family) can be expected to make a larger contribution toward college costs. By the third year, the student has a much better measure of likely success in completing a four-year or longer course of study, and education often tends to become more career oriented; thus, the risks of failure to complete college are much less and the potential rewards of personal investment in further education are significantly higher. As a student approaches age 20, the opportunities for summer employment improve, there are greater possibilities for combining work and study, and borrowing against future earnings is a much less risky decision. The Panel on Student Financial Need Analysis, asked by the College Scholarship Service in 1969 to review the philosophy of college scholarship policy, recommended "need-related aid with threshold preference"—that is, highest priority for grant aid to lower-division students with financial need, with rising expectations of self-help (parents, jobs, loans) as a student approaches the degree goal (College Entrance Examination Board, 1971).

The Commission believes that this goal might appropriately be incorporated into tuition policy as well, with student charges for lower-division, upper-division, and graduate studies more nearly reflecting the differential instructional costs of these levels of education. As a rough rule of thumb we envisage public tuition levels on the average over the next decade moving toward a level equal to about one-third of educational costs.[5]

Recommendation 5: Public colleges and universities should carefully study their educational costs per student and consider restructuring their tuition charges at upper-division and graduate levels to more nearly reflect the real differences in the cost of education per student, eventually reaching a general level equal to about one-third of educational costs.

The combined effect of Recommendations 4 and 5 would result in a more equitable sharing of the costs among students at various levels.

---

[5] The State University of New York implemented a policy in 1972 that approximated this goal, with charges in the senior institutions set at $650 for freshmen and sophomores, $800 for upperclassmen, $1,200 for graduate students, and $1,600 for professional students. This one-third level, as we noted earlier, is generally consistent with a distribution of economic costs—two-thirds to students and their families, and one-third to government sources and philanthropy.

Recommendation 6: Private colleges and universities should increase their tuition charges at a rate that is no more rapid than the increase in per capita disposable income. The rate of increase in tuition should be less pronounced than this, if at all possible.

Recommendation 7: Private colleges and universities also should carefully study their educational costs per student and consider restructuring their tuition charges, so that tuition is relatively low for lower-division students, somewhat higher for upper-division students, and considerably higher for graduate and professional students.

BASIC OPPORTUNITY GRANTS The Basic Opportunity Grants program authorized under the Higher Education Act of 1972 in its original form would have reimbursed needy students for the cost of education up to a maximum of $1,400, but emerged from the House/Senate conference with a maximum grant of $1,400, *provided* the grant did not exceed 50 percent of cost. This means that the student who needs full support will receive not more than one-half of that amount under the federal program, whereas under full funding some students whose families can contribute one-half of the expense may receive the full amount of their residual "need."[6] While the Commission recognizes that the conferees may have had legitimate reasons to limit the amount of funds for the basic grants program, it believes that this limitation unduly penalizes the student from a very poor family.

The limitation of the maximum award to $1,400 less parental contribution also means that the lower-middle income student attending a high-tuition private college would receive little or no assistance. For instance, if the total cost of attending college is $4,400—a not uncommon figure today—and the parental contribution is only one-third of that amount ($1,400), the student

[6] Under the BOG program the student may receive an amount equal to the difference between the cost of attending college and the expected parental contribution, with the maximum award limited to (a) 50 percent of the total cost or (b) $1,400, whichever is smaller. Thus if the cost of college is $1,400, the students with 100 percent need and 50 percent need would each receive $700. Under the less than full funding of the act, however, no student can receive more than 50 to 60 percent of the difference between his need and the actual cost of attendance.

receives no award although his need is substantial ($3,000). This is because no student can receive an amount more than $1,400 less the expected parental contribution.

The Basic Opportunity Grants program is a major step in the direction of removing the financial obstacle to access to college, but we feel that three actions should be taken by the Administration and the Congress as soon as possible:

Recommendation 8: The Basic Opportunity Grants program should be fully funded. This legislation, already on the books, is a major step in providing critically needed assistance to both students and institutions of higher education.

Recommendation 9: In keeping with the principles elaborated under Recommendations 4 and 7 above, the 50 percent of cost limitation for Basic Opportunity Grants for lower-division students should be raised, perhaps in steps, to 75 percent over the next few years.

Recommendation 10: The Commission also recommends that in the future the $1,400 ceiling on Basic Opportunity Grants be raised gradually in line with increases in educational and subsistence costs.

We believe that these three recommendations would create a national program of student assistance that would move us significantly toward the achievement of the goal of universal access to higher education.

We recognize that our recommendations would not enable a needy residential student to meet his full costs at a typical private college, but the restructuring of tuition charges that we have recommended would ease the situation for lower-division students. For the upper-division student, we recommend relatively greater reliance on loans or deferred-tuition plans. A number of leading private institutions have been restructuring their aid policies in this direction in recent years, though generally without the distinction we have suggested between lower-division and upper-division students.

With federal grants limited to a fraction of the total cost of attending college even for the most needy student, we believe that state scholarship programs should be encouraged to make up the difference, particularly in the first two years of post-secondary education. The maximum award under state scholarship programs might be designed to cover up to 25 percent of the cost of attending a public institution.

Thus, in a state college or university the student with no family resources would have his or her minimal needs met for the lower-division years (75 percent federal, 25 percent state aid), and the upper-division student would have three-fourths of his or her tuition and subsistence costs met (50 percent from federal sources, 25 percent state). Self-help from employment and loans would be expected to meet a rising fraction of the cost as the student progressed from lower-division to upper-division to postgraduate study.

If the federal Basic Opportunity Grants program is limited to a fraction of total cost, we believe that the federal government should take the responsibility of assuring that all states are encouraged to assume their share of providing supplemental support for the student without adequate resources. Under the Higher Education Act of 1972 (Section 415) federal funds are authorized (but not yet appropriated) to match incremental state student incentive awards. This would represent a major first step by the federal government to encourage state efforts, but it penalizes states that have already embarked on significant state scholarship programs. We believe that the 50–50 matching of *incremental* funds should eventually be replaced by perhaps a 25 percent federal contribution toward the cost of all state incentive awards, providing that state programs are primarily based upon need and are sufficient to cover unmet needs of the low-income student in the first two years of attendance at a public college.

Recommendation 11: The federal government should appropriate full funding for state student incentive matching grants. We also recommend that the federal program be modified in the next several years to provide one-fourth of all state awards that meet the criterion of making up, for students with full need, the difference between federal Basic Opportunity Grants and the full cost of attending college in the first two years at public institutions, and a significant fraction of the difference in upper-division years. The awards would be reduced by appropriate amounts for students with less than full need.

Perhaps the most perplexing problem facing higher education today is the diminishing capacity of private institutions to survive in the face of the wide tuition gap at the undergraduate level and a marked slowing down in the rate of growth of college enrollments. We believe it is essential for the health of our total educational system that the great majority of private colleges and universities are not permitted to decline in quality. Enrolling about one-fourth of all students in the country, they provide diverse educational options for students, and they perform a valuable role in quality education, curricular reform and innovation, teaching methods, and research. They also play an exceedingly valuable role in professional and graduate education and research.

Several principles guide our recommendations concerning the private sector of higher education:

1   To the extent that higher education represents a public benefit, societal advantages accrue from attendance at a private college just as from attending a public college. Thus the issue of public support of higher education should not be decided only on the principle of governance and administrative control.

2   Independent institutions are important resources in the regions in which they are located, and state governments should assume greater responsibility for the effect upon these institutions of decisions made for the public sector. Thus, particularly when setting tuition policies in public institutions, state agencies should take into consideration the impact of this decision upon the private colleges and universities.

3   The federal government has traditionally treated public and private institutions similarly as institutions serving the public interest, and has held each equally accountable to performance standards. Accountability as to performance need not be synonymous with control, nor must accountability presume identical standards for all institutions. Private institutions add diversity to the system precisely because many of them differ from their public counterparts—in class size, teaching methods, facilities, and programs—and public support should not erase these differing patterns. Governmental support should always require accountability, but minimal controls.

4   The largest component of our system of higher education today

consists of public colleges and universities, and their traditional strength and dedication to service to their community should not be curtailed. Public agencies should strive to create a climate in which public and private institutions reinforce and complement each other's strength, and avoid weakening either at the other's expense.

In keeping with these principles, the Commission believes that several interrelated steps should be taken by federal and state governments and by institutions. The first step is the full funding of the Basic Opportunity Grants program, which will aid all collegiate institutions both public and private. The second is the recommendation that the 50 percent of cost limitation for lower-division students be gradually raised to 75 percent. Third is the federal matching of state incentive grant programs. These developments would permit the states to alter their tuition policies in a manner that would reverse the trend toward a steadily widening gap between public and private institutions.

The fact that the Basic Opportunity Grants program has been designed to meet a certain proportion of the students' full costs, including both tuition and subsistence, means that the cost-of-education supplements recommended earlier by the Commission may no longer be necessary.[7] We had intended the Educational Opportunity Grants we recommended, with a maximum award of $1,000, to cover subsistence costs only, and had proposed cost-of-education supplements as a means of assisting colleges and universities in holding down their tuition charges.

STATE POLICIES   Recommendation 12: We recommend that state governments take positive steps toward a gradual narrowing of the tuition differential between public and private institutions in their jurisdictions. This can be accomplished through adjustments in tuition levels at public institutions with an accompanying statewide program of student aid that will minimize the cost to the low-income student, by a program of direct or indirect support to private institutions to enable them to keep tuition charges from rising unduly rapidly, or by a combination of both.

[7]See *Quality and Equality Revised* (1970c, Sec. 7).

Subsidies to private institutions, which now exist under programs enacted in several states, may be a less costly means of assisting the movement toward universal access to higher education than complete reliance upon the continued expansion of the public sector. As we have argued above, to the extent there are public benefits from the provision of public higher education at tuition charges far below cost, these external benefits also accrue from collegiate education in private institutions. Although we have no precise way of measuring the magnitude of these societal benefits, we presume them to be substantial. If we were to set outer limits, we would urge that institutional subsidies to private institutions not be greater than about one-fifth of the educational costs for undergraduate education in a counterpart public institution.[8] Such levels of institutional aid are generally in keeping with our view that the overall pattern of support should continue to expect about one-third of the total monetary outlay and two-thirds of economic costs to be met by students and parents. If state aid reaches these proportions, we believe it is appropriate for the state to require that some

---

[8] Educational costs at private institutions average about 15 percent higher than at public institutions. Since these extra costs are presumably the basis for extra benefits, we believe they should be borne by the students one way or another. This adjustment having been made, public and private costs may be assumed to be equal. Educational costs of private institutions are now subsidized about 40 percent from several sources (more than half of the amount is a direct or indirect burden on public sources); and tuition covers 60 percent. We have suggested that public tuition rise to one-third of educational costs. This leaves a gap of about 27 percentage points (60 percent less one-third) between costs covered by private tuition, net of extra benefits, and public tuition. Thus, with a maximum public subsidy per student at private colleges of about one-fifth of the educational costs at a comparable public institution, the private institution would be receiving a subsidy amounting to about 30 percent of the subsidy received by a comparable public institution (20 percent of educational costs compared with $66^2/_3$ percent of educational costs). In addition, a substantial subsidy from public sources is already reflected in the "private subsidy" at private institutions, as we have noted above. Thus, our proposal would bring total student subsidies—from both public and private sources—at private institutions almost up to those for public institutions in terms of comparable costs (not including the "extra costs" of private institutions noted above).

It should be noted, however, that while tuition covers about 60 percent of educational costs in the average private institution, there are many private colleges that have virtually no endowment and are almost entirely dependent on tuition to meet their costs of education. These colleges are forced to keep their costs of education as low as possible to avoid raising tuition excessively. They would be especially aided by a state subsidy.

proportion of these institutional funds be used to assist low- and middle-income level students in meeting the costs of attending college. We believe it would be particularly appropriate if such funds could be used primarily to lower the cost of attending college in the first two years, along the lines of the restructuring of tuition levels in private institutions envisaged in Recommendation 7.

There are several formulas by which direct aid is now given to private institutions. In New York and Maryland it is based upon degrees awarded; FTE enrollments at various levels of education are the determinants in North Carolina and Illinois; in Pennsylvania it has been a negotiable grant based on a number of factors of state service. State grants based upon enrollment can more easily distinguish between lower- and upper-division enrollments and thus provide greater flexibility for state policy. For example, if it were determined that a portion of state aid should be used for tuition remission at the lower-division level, an enrollment-based grant formula would be more appropriate for this purpose. Aid formulas based upon number of degrees awarded may create undue incentives to award degrees and place too much emphasis upon the outcome rather than the educational experience.

We recognize that various states have different historic traditions, different current patterns in the balance of public and private higher education, and different constitutional, political, and financial factors that may affect the state's long-term policy goal and the speed with which it is implemented. A policy appropriate for New Mexico or Wyoming, which have practically no private sector, obviously may be quite different from that which seems appropriate in Vermont or Massachusetts, where private higher education still predominates.

We believe that experimentation with different patterns of direct subsidy to public and private institutions, and varying combinations of direct student aid and tuition policy, state by state, is a healthy development. This would provide a diversity of experience that will be useful in developing guidelines for effective educational policy in the future.

The preference of the Commission, nevertheless, as we have noted earlier, is for grants-in-aid based upon the need of the student. Such grants would cover the cost of attending public institutions when there is full need by the student, taking into account federal aid. At private institutions they would cover this amount and the additional public subsidy at a comparable public institution (or the private tuition if it is lower than this combination where there is full need by the student). We see no good reason why the tuition grant to attend a private college should be greater than the student cost and additional public subsidy at a comparable public institution even if the tuition at the private institution exceeds these two amounts.

The Commission sees the issues of tuition levels in the public sector, the possible subsidy of education in private colleges and universities, and the magnitude of state student-aid programs as necessarily interdependent—a public policy decision in any one area is interrelated with the other two. Thus, a state that chooses to maintain a low-tuition level in public institutions would need a somewhat smaller-than-average state student-aid program, but might need to introduce or expand direct institutional aid to private colleges and universities. At the other extreme, a state that pursues a policy of increasing public tuition very greatly would not need to provide substantial aid to private institutions, but it would have to have a significant student-aid program. Equity and ease of access can be effectively served under either alternative.

We propose as a preferred path the gradual increase of tuition charges in public institutions over the next decade or so toward one-third of the cost of education, with a corresponding increase in student aid based upon need at both public and private institutions because we believe that in addition to serving the goals of equality of opportunity and universal access, this would help to:

Broaden the range of institutional choice for students

Create a better climate for coexistence of public and private institutions

Complement the new federal philosophy of aid to low-income students

Promise most effective use from limited state tax revenues

The one-third of educational cost proposal for public institutions is consistent with our view that in the long run the public/private share of total economic costs should be approximately one-third–two-thirds (including forgone earnings).

The task of accommodating additional enrollment, which by the early 1980s will be 30 to 40 percent greater than in 1970, partly arising from the growth in the college-age group and partly from making equality of educational opportunity a reality, should not be placed entirely upon the shoulders of the taxpayer. We believe that the historic sharing of the cost burden between public and private sources that has emerged is an appropriate one, and reasonably well reflects the balance of individual and societal benefits from higher education.

If the recommended gradual redistribution of costs among families from various income levels does not occur through compensating adjustments in student charges and financial aid, then to accomplish the same societal goals would (1) require a more rapid increase in the government share to aid the low-income entrants to higher education, (2) leave the private colleges and universities in an increasingly difficult competitive position, and (3) increase even more rapidly the proportion of total enrollment in the state-supported institutions with a further escalation of public costs. We believe these are unnecessary and undesirable trends, and strongly prefer to see the present balance of public and private support for higher education maintained, with redistribution of the public support more in accordance with ability to pay.

LOAN POLICIES Debates over the issue of tuition levels often confuse two questions: *What* can one afford to pay? *When* can one afford to pay? In light of our proposals for institutional pricing policy and public student-aid programs, significant numbers of students will need to borrow—or otherwise defer tuition and subsistence costs—to meet part of their educational needs. If higher education is to move toward a pricing policy that places more reliance upon ability to pay, it will require both a generous grant program and a fully adequate loan program. The first step in the direction of an adequate grant program has been taken with the Higher Education Act of 1972; it is our judgment, however, that we are losing ground in developing a loan program adequate to the task.

In *Quality and Equality, Revised,* we outlined our proposals for the development of a National Student Loan Bank to make long-term loans (of 20 to 30 years) with repayments partly contingent upon current earnings (Carnegie Commission on Higher Education, 1970*c*, pp. 9–13). Low-tuition public colleges provide a local option for most students, but we believe it strongly desirable to broaden the range of options and add to the student's mobility by providing ample loan funds to enable attendance at a residential public or private college or university. The creation of an adequate capital market for borrowing for advanced education is, we believe, an important responsibility of the federal government.

In contrast with the loan program recommended by the Commission, the major existing federal loan program is the Guaranteed Loan Program, under which private lenders (chiefly commercial banks) provide loans to students and are guaranteed against default through an insurance program of the federal government. There is a ceiling on the interest rate that may be charged, which at times has restricted the supply of available loan funds to considerably less than the demand (Hartman, 1971, Ch. 4). Students are not charged interest during periods of enrollment or military service. Lenders are reimbursed for this lost interest by the federal government—that is, the loans are subsidized. The repayment period is the 10 years following completion of the student's program of study. There are limitations on the amounts that can be borrowed, which were liberalized by the Higher Education Act of 1972. The act also established the Student Loan Marketing Association to provide a secondary market for loans, similar to the secondary mortgage market provided by the Federal National Mortgage Association.

Studies of high school and college graduates clearly show that the absolute differential in earnings that is associated with added educational experience tends to widen significantly over one's lifetime, and that the average college graduate assumes family responsibilities earlier in his working career than does his high school counterpart. An ideal loan program would adjust the costs of repayment to the lifetime flow of benefits, and would make allowance for family costs, thus concentrating the repayment burden on borrowers at a time when they can expect to reap the most significant benefit from this investment. Traditional loan concepts, borrowed from the world of commerce and industry where physical plant suffers from depreciation and obsolescence, are not equally appropriate to investment in human capital.

We do not favor forgiveness features in federally sponsored

loan programs, believing that they tend to distort remuneration policies in the favored "public service" employments, and that they unduly distinguish between borrowers on the one hand and students who either receive sufficient need-based grants-in-aid or take jobs to finance their education on the other. Nor do we believe it is wise policy to waive interest charges during the period a student is in school; rather we would recommend that such charges be deferred and amortized over the life of the loan. Under present waiver conditions elaborate institutional machinery and policing is necessary to prevent abuse of this privilege, and it takes only a few instances of interest-free borrowing on the part of students for reinvestment purposes while they are still enrolled as students to discredit the entire loan program. Without the waiver of interest charges while still enrolled in school, forgiveness features, or interest subsidization, there would be no need to enforce strict rules about demonstrating need to achieve loan eligibility. We believe that the creation of an adequate capital market, with minimal restrictions upon its use, would go far to ease the implementation of the recommendations we have made as regards tuition policies.

Criticism is sometimes leveled at income-contingent repayment programs because the woman who borrows to help pay college costs may take a "negative dowry" into marriage. We believe that this argument is less persuasive than it might at first appear, particularly as the proportion of college-educated women in the labor force continues to rise. At the present time, about 50 percent of the women with one or more years of college are in the labor force, and the proportions are considerably higher than this for female college graduates and holders of advanced degrees. Even in the case of a woman who does not hold employment outside the household because of dependents, provision can be made, as is done in Sweden, to prevent an undue burden on a low-income family. For example, if both the husband and wife have borrowed while in college, and their income is below some minimum (say $7,500), the scheduled repayment of one spouse might be deferred; at an income of $15,000 or above, the full repayment for both would be charged currently against their joint income (even if one were not employed). Experience with traditional loans, even with the relatively short repayment schedule, suggests that women themselves value education sufficiently to assume the risks of borrowing if necessary. A contingent loan program, with the suggested modifications, would be much less burdensome than the options that are now available to women.

A contingent loan program with flexible long-term repayment provisions, such as we have recommended, could easily be handled as part of the annual federal income tax return. An insurance feature could be built in to protect against death or disability, or short-term economic reversal of fortunes. Unlike the Educational Opportunity Bank proposal made by the Panel on Educational Innovation (1967), we see the National Student Loan Bank as a means of providing supplementary funding for students, not as a way of financing total educational costs. Our proposal also assumes eventual full repayment of loans by the individual (with exceptions in the event of catastrophe), rather than a sharing among borrowers of lifetime income risks that has been a feature of several other proposals. We believe that our recommended program would do much to ease the burden of college costs on students and families at all income levels, and would be in keeping with the trend toward greater responsibility being assumed by students for their own education.

Recommendation 13: The Commission once again urges that the federal government charter a National Student Loan Bank as a nonprofit corporation financed by the sale of governmentally guaranteed securities, which would serve all eligible students regardless of need. The fund should be self-sustaining, except for catastrophic risks, and should permit borrowing up to a reasonable limit that would reflect both tuition charges and subsistence costs. Loan repayments should be based upon income currently earned, and up to 40 years should be permitted for repayment. Provision should be made for public subsidy of catastrophic risks.

COST ESTIMATES   The estimated cost to the federal government of fully implementing the BOG program, with the modification that we have recommended in the cost limitation for lower-division students, ranges from about $1.7 to $2.3 billion, depending on how many "extra" students, who would not otherwise enroll, are induced to attend college because of the existence of the program.[9] The total cost in current dollars might be expected to rise some 60 to 70 percent above these levels by 1980, depending on future increases in enrollment and in costs per FTE student, as well as on the willingness of Congress to adjust the maximum award to cost increases.[10]

The estimated federal cost of the State Student Incentive matching grants, with the federal government contributing 25 percent of the state award, is about $120 million for fiscal year 1973–74. The cost to the states would be about $360 million, but this would represent an increase of only about $170 million over 1969–70 state expenditures for scholarship programs.[11] As in the case of the Basic Opportunity Grants, these costs might be expected to rise some 60 to 70 percent by 1980, depending on the behavior of enrollment and of the cost of education.

---

[9] These estimates are adapted from the carefully developed cost estimates prepared by Hartman (1972*b*) for the Joint Economic Committee, U.S. Congress.

[10] Enrollment has been rising considerably less rapidly in the last several years than projections based on past trends had indicated (see Carnegie Commission, 1973, Chart 14). Whether this trend will continue through the 1970s is unclear, but, if it does, the increase in undergraduate enrollment in the 1970s may turn out to be only about 30 to 40 percent, as compared with the 50 percent increase suggested by our projections (see Carnegie Commission, 1971*c*, Appendix Table 8).

The Commission's earlier recommendation for educational opportunity grants was estimated to involve costs of $1.3 billion in 1970–71; $2.3 billion in 1976–77; and $2.7 billion in 1979–80 in constant dollars (Carnegie Commission, 1970*c*, pp. 32–33). Our present estimate of the cost of BOG grants in 1980 suggests a range of from $2.2 to $3.2 billion in constant dollars. Our earlier recommendation was less costly in recommending a maximum grant of $1,000, rather than of $1,400, but was more costly in proposing a federal program of grants for needy graduate students in their first two years of graduate work. We now believe, especially in view of the lowering of the age of adulthood, that a needs test for graduate students would be exceedingly difficult to administer, and that there should be relatively increased emphasis on loans as the predominant form of student aid in the early years of graduate education. Also, the cost-of-education supplements that we had recommended are now, in effect but only in part, incorporated within the Basic Opportunity Grants, and we had estimated they might cost over $3 billion by 1980.

[11] These estimates were also adapted from Hartman (1972*b*, p. 481).

15. Who Does What?

The adjustments that we envisage over the next 10 years to make universal access a reality and to ensure greater equity will require the concerted action of federal and state governments, and of both public and private institutions. Our recommendations for the most part are in keeping with recent trends in the financing of higher education, and would provide an orderly path toward national objectives. The necessary steps over the next decade can be summarized as follows:

THE FEDERAL GOVERNMENT By virtue of its perspective, encompassing national educational goals and attainment, the federal government plays a critical initiatory role. The Higher Education Act of 1972 represents a significant advance in principle, although its implementation may be slower than originally anticipated. Over the course of the decade the priorities for federal action are:

Full funding of existing student-aid legislation, particularly the Basic Opportunity Grants program

Increasing the BOG maximum award gradually in future years to reflect increases in student costs

The extension, as soon as practical, of the ceiling on BOG awards to 75 percent of the student cost for lower-division education

Extension of the federal matching provisions to state scholarship programs to 25 percent of expenditure, provided that state programs appropriately supplement federal BOG awards

Stabilization of federal support for graduate education at a reasonable long-term level, and the establishment of a comprehensive doctoral fellowship program with selection based upon demonstrated academic ability

Gradual increases in the funding of sponsored research approximately matching the growth in the GNP

Establishment of a national student loan bank to provide long-term student loans with repayment contingent upon income

These steps would gradually raise the federal share to approximately 50 percent of total governmental funding of higher education, and would finally remove the financial barriers to postsecondary education for students from low-income backgrounds in all 50 states. Federal action would also provide the incentive for adjustments in state and institutional policy that will be required to accomplish the goal of universal access.

STATE GOVERNMENTS State governments, as the largest source of institutional support for higher education, play a vital role in any gradual redistribution of the burden of college costs. Being closer to their constituencies, and having traditionally been the chief public agencies that have provided the facilities and institutional organization of systems of higher education, state governments give form and substance to the assurance of educational opportunity. Our recommendations encourage the following state actions:

Assume greater responsibility for the well-being of all higher education within their boundaries, recognizing that private colleges and universities provide public benefits similar in nature and magnitude to those of state or municipal colleges and universities

Reform state tax systems to make them more progressive, thus providing greater equity in the financing of education and other public services

Provide adequate support to public institutions to maintain the quality of programs and to accommodate all students who can benefit from postsecondary education and training

Through funding formulas for public institutions, assure that tuition charges for the first two years of postsecondary education are not beyond the means of students from low-income families

Enable students of limited means to attend either public or private colleges by developing a comprehensive student-assistance program that adequately supplements federal programs

Support action to narrow gradually the tuition gap between public and private institutions through tuition adjustments in public colleges and universities

Provide modest, direct, institutional aid to private colleges and universities, and/or tuition grants that take into account higher tuition at private institutions

The cooperation of institutions of higher education is essential to make sure that national and state objectives are achieved. The primary adjustment anticipated over the coming decade is a gradual revision in tuition policy, and the close coordination of institutional student-assistance programs with developing federal and state programs.

We have recommended that public institutions:

Carefully study their educational cost with an eye to adjusting their tuition charges to more nearly reflect real differences in cost by level of education, and particularly to make charges for the first two years of college as low as is feasible

Cooperate in a gradual change in pricing philosophy which would permit tuition levels to rise gradually to about one-third of educational costs, assuming that federal, state, and institutional student-aid resources keep pace so that students in need of assistance are not barred from access to postsecondary education

Private colleges and universities are urged to:

Consider the advisability of charging differential tuitions by level of education, as in the case of public institutions, and use institutional student-aid funds to effectively offset a larger proportion of the costs of attending college for the first two years and assume increasing self-help on the part of students in upper-division and graduate studies

Insofar as is possible in keeping with the maintenance of quality of programs, to limit increases in tuition charges to not more (and preferably less) than the proportionate increase in per capita disposable income

In the case of all institutions, public and private, the Commission urges restraint in expenditures, and redoubled efforts to assure the most effective use of resources consistent with the maintenance of quality.

Our recommendations do not propose any specific action on the part of students and their families, but the adjustments we envisage in tuition and student-assistance policies will gradually change the perceptions and expectations of individuals as "consumers" of education. Over the period of the next decade or so we anticipate that:

A larger proportion of college students will come from economically disadvantaged backgrounds

They will be enabled to attend college by a significant expansion of federal and state programs of student aid

Tuition charges in public institutions will rise more rapidly than in the past

Tuition charges in private institutions will rise at about the rate of increase in per capita disposable income (somewhat more slowly than in the recent past)

Students, and their parents, who can afford to pay will have to shoulder a larger proportion of educational costs, but low-income students will be enabled to meet subsistence as well as tuition costs

The principle of increasing self-help as one progresses through college will become more common, and beyond the lower-division years students may have to depend somewhat more heavily upon loan financing

Thus, the net effect of our recommendations in the longer run is to maintain the proportion of total monetary outlays on higher education borne by students and their families at about one-third (two-thirds of total economic costs, including forgone incomes), but to aid students from low-income backgrounds by requiring a proportionate increase in the share borne by those from more affluent families. For the next few years, however, as an increasing proportion of youth from low-income families gain the financial means to afford college, the taxpayer share of the monetary outlay on higher education will rise modestly; but it will then drop again. In our view, the interests of equity are better served by this gradual redistribution of burdens, and in this manner the nation can more rapidly move toward equalization of educational opportunities.

The Commission shares the concern of many observers of the college scene about the continued long-run health of private institutions. Our recommendation that there be a gradual and modest redistribution of the cost burden among families, so that those who can afford to contribute more assist in freeing resources for use in aiding students from disadvantaged backgrounds, has the added advantage of promoting an environment in which the private college or university has a better chance to achieve financial stability. Our recommendations would assist private institutions in the following manner:

By gradually narrowing the tuition gap between public and private colleges, and returning the tuition ratio more nearly to its historic level in the period 1920 to 1950

Through greatly increased student-assistance programs that permit the needy student to choose more equally between attendance at a public or private college, and that help institutions to reduce their student-aid deficit

By stabilizing the support of graduate education, and gradually improving research funding, so that in both public and private universities graduate study and research needs do not divert funds from undergraduate education

Through the creation of an adequate loan program with long-term income-contingent repayment provisions assisting students in meeting current educational costs

These recommendations do not guarantee that all private colleges and universities will improve their position, but we believe that they create conditions whereby the well-administered private institution that performs a distinctive educational service can compete with tax-supported institutions on a more equitable basis. In a period like the forthcoming decade or two, when continuous growth is likely to give way to conditions more like that of the steady state, some private institutions may indeed not survive. However, we believe that our recommendations make it probable that the private higher educational sector can retain its share of total enrollment, and continue to serve the public interest as it has done historically.

In conclusion, several cautionary notes concerning the implementation of our recommendations should be reiterated. First, we have indicated the *direction* in which we believe public policy should move during the decade, but caution should be observed in the *speed* with which the shift in the funding patterns is effected. Private tuition levels increased at an annual average rate of 6.9 percent from 1960 to 1972; this was slightly more rapid than the 5.8 percent increase in disposable income levels, and we believe it must slow down. Public tuition levels, on the other hand, rose 5.3 percent annually over the decade, but the average dollar increase was quite small ($21 a year in the 1967–68 to 1971–72 period, compared with $140 for the private sector). If average tuition levels in the public sector for state residents are to rise from 15 percent of educational costs in 1970[1] to approximately one-third in the early 1980s, this would mean an average annual increase in the decade equal to about 10 to 12 percent—a somewhat higher rate than has been experienced in the recent past. Some states or institutions will prefer to make these changes in two or three steps rather than annually, and care must be taken to ensure that students with financial need are not unduly penalized or discouraged from attending college.

The second cautionary note is that *tuition increases in the public sector must be accompanied by compensating increases in student aid and loan funds* or ground will be lost in assuring universal access. At least the lowest-income one-third (and preferably one-half) of students must be no worse off than under the current low-tuition/low-student-aid pattern, and those at the lowest-income end of the scale should be sufficiently better off to remove all financial obstacles to attendance. States would do a disservice by adopting only the tuition adjustment recommendations without ensuring that student-aid programs adequately met existing needs.

Third, *state policy must keep in step with federal action in funding basic student-aid programs*. The Higher Education Act of 1972 is an important first step in this direction, and the full funding of the Basic Opportunity Grants program must be the first priority. Our recommendations presume a further broadening of federal student assistance during the remainder of this decade. This task will be made somewhat easier as veterans' educational benefits, at their peak in 1973, gradually phase down over the next five years, thus releasing funds for other programs. However, states will understandably be limited in their response if federal action is inadequate.

And, finally, the Commission recognizes that *its recommendations on financing*, while perhaps adequate to the present and

---

[1] Total tuition and fee income, from both in-state and out-of-state students, averaged 17 percent of educational income of public institutions in 1970-71 (Table 4).

near future, *may need further modification in light of the evolving social and legal milieu.* If the trend toward earlier "emancipation" of students brings about a decline in parental responsibility, greater attention will have to be given to the means of assuring opportunities for student self-help. Despite the adoption in many states of age 18 as the legal age of majority and the several court decisions on state residence requirements, we believe that the changes will be evolutionary and that parental resources will remain a primary source of student support for many years to come.

Our proposals have concentrated primarily on undergraduate education, largely because the issues of equity and the extent of societal benefits (as contrasted with personal benefits) are more clearly evident at that level. At graduate and advanced professional levels the benefits are predominantly private (although this is not necessarily true of basic research, which is often performed in conjunction with graduate education), awards are based more upon talent than upon family resources, and the student is in a better position to borrow against future earnings or to combine employment and study. Recommendations about aid at postbaccalaureate levels are contained in several earlier reports (see Carnegie Commission, *Quality and Equality, Revised, The More Effective Use of Resources, Higher Education and the Nation's Health*).

This report only touches on several other important areas of concern—postsecondary education in noncollegiate settings and recurrent educational opportunities throughout life—not because we believe them to be less important, but because they are the subject of a forthcoming Commission report. While a majority of the nation's youth now have some college experience in the immediate post-high school years, increasing recognition is being given today to the less traditional forms and patterns of postsecondary education. The extension of educational opportunity throughout one's lifetime, and through a variety of diverse learning experiences, is a next major step in the evolution of our society, and the Commission's attention will be devoted to this less well-charted area in a future report.

With the end of the Vietnam war, we urge all levels of government, and most particularly the President and the Congress, to place the improved funding of higher education once again high on their agenda. We have come close to achieving the goal of universal access to higher education, and we have made substantial strides in providing greater equality of opportunity. A significant forward step was taken with the passage of the Higher Education Act of 1972, representing a new vision of the federal role in assuring access to postsecondary education for those with inadequate family resources. The first item on the nation's educational agenda must now be the full funding of existing legislation. Beyond that, we have proposed a series of steps both for federal and state action that we believe will serve well the nation's educational needs in the 1970s and into the 1980s. Building on the start already made, a more equitable and more sensible system of financing higher education can be created to make better connections between those who benefit and those who pay.

Appendix A: The Consolidated Institutional Income Accounts and Alternative Ways of Viewing the Cost Burden of Higher Education

Discussions of the share of educational costs borne by users, taxpayers, and others suffer from inconsistencies in the definition of costs. In this report we have attempted to create a historical series of aggregate institutional accounts that is consistently reported and have used several special definitions of educational income and cost (see Glossary, pp. 26–27). The data presented here, and summarized in the text, provide a useful view of major trends in the financing of higher education.

Appendix A draws on studies done for the Carnegie Commission by June O'Neill. In *Resource Use in Higher Education* (1971) she has developed an alternate-year series of expenditure accounts for higher education dating back to 1929–30. In her report, *Sources of Funds to Colleges and Universities* (1973), she similarly reports income data through 1967–68. These series have been updated by Commission staff through 1970–71, with preliminary figures for 1971–72.

In Tables A-1 through A-13 institutional income items have been assigned to one of four columns to reflect the incidence of these costs to families, taxpayers, philanthropy, and others. However, a number of adjustments are necessary to obtain cost measures that are relevant to the assessment of trends and public policy determination.

The usual institutional accounts include a number of items that have little to do with the educational function of colleges and universities, and the subtraction of "noneducational services" is an attempt to remove the service expenditures that are not directly related to education. Deducted to obtain Total Educational Funds of Institutions are: 75 percent of federally funded research and services, all amounts under Sale of Services (which are essentially services performed for noncampus users), income from Related Activities (which includes income from real estate, athletic events, adult nondegree programs, special short courses contracted for by external agencies, and a variety of extracurricular affairs), Student-Aid Income (which is incorporated in the lower section under "Adjustments"), Auxiliary-Enterprise income assumed to originate from students and the 7 percent assumed to come from nonstudents.

The division of research income is a somewhat arbitrary one. We have assumed that approximately one-fourth of federally sponsored research activities are so closely intertwined with the educational process that if those funds were not provided under research contracts they would have to be obtained from some alternative source to provide the same educational services. In fact, when such funds contract or disappear altogether, as has been fairly common in the last several years, universities are likely to be thrown into a deficit position and then have to curtail expenditures in other areas as a partial compensation. Included in the 25 percent of research funds not subtracted are such items as the partial support of computers, library acquisitions, laboratory equipment and supplies, graduate student assistance, and some fraction of professorial salaries. An alternative way of expressing our assumption would be to say that three-fourths of sponsored research activity at universities could conceivably be contracted for with noneducational agencies—nonprofit research institutes, private or municipal hospitals, private firms, or individual researchers. It may be convenient for universities to perform these research services—and we believe that the social benefits of university research outweigh their direct costs—but not all such activities are an integral part of educational activities. (See Appendix B).

The resulting subtotal, showing the total flow of funds through institutional accounts that can be identified as educational income, better reflects the real cost of educational services and the share of costs borne by the four categories of income source.

However, if we are primarily concerned with the real burden on families, taxpayers, and philanthropy, some further adjustments must be made. Under "Adjustments," student-aid expenditures from all sources are deducted from the family contribution. Added back into the taxpayer and philanthropic accounts are the income items deducted under "noneducational services," plus estimated amounts that do not pass through the institutional accounts—predominantly veterans' benefits and social security payments to dependents in college and direct scholarship awards to students by foundations and other private agencies. It should be noted that the amount deducted from family outlays is larger than the sum of amounts added in the next two columns. The difference is the contribution from current funds of colleges and universities. Table A-14 estimates total student-aid funds by source and shows the derivation of the amounts under this heading in Tables A-1 through A-13.

Estimated student expenditures for basic living costs are added to family costs under "Adjustments." It is estimated that in 1970–71 approximately $1,200 was spent per student in residence on room, board, books, and supplies, and about $850 per student not housed in institutional facilities. These amounts were adjusted by use of cost-of-living indexes to estimate expenditures in earlier years. The subsistence estimates are conservative, reflecting only the essential minimum costs of college attendance.

Total Monetary Outlay on Education by families, taxpayers, and private philanthropy is a useful cost definition when discussing matters of equity, for it more accurately shows the direct cost burden for each type of contributor.

Finally, net forgone income (net of subsistence costs already included above) is added to family costs to determine Total Economic Cost. Estimates of forgone income in recent years are based on a Commission study done by Walt McKibben. Hourly income for the average student enrolled in 1966 was found to be 93 percent of the average hourly earnings in manufacturing, and this ratio was assumed to hold true for each of the other years. (See pp. 49–53 above for a more complete description of the estimates.) Total economic cost perhaps best reflects the real economic sacrifice made by each category of income source.

Table A-14 shows our estimate of student-aid expenditures, by category, for 1929–30, 1939–40, and for alternate years beginning with 1949–50. This was perhaps the most difficult figure to come by, for aggregate student-aid expenditures are never reported in this fashion. Only about 40 percent of such grant-in-aid funds passes through the usually reported institutional accounts. In recent years veterans' benefits to college students and social security dependents' benefits have constituted about

50 percent of the total, and direct grants from state governments and nonprofit agencies make up another estimated 10 percent. Our estimates do not include graduate students supported on research assistantships, which some might argue are in most cases akin to doctoral fellowships. (See Table 29 for an estimate at graduate student assistance.)

Column 6 of Table A-14 shows the difference between student-aid income and total student-aid expenditures reported by institutions. This figure is often referred to as "the student-aid deficit," representing a drain on current general funds. Column 7 is an estimate of student aid going directly to students from business firms, churches, foundations, Kiwanis Clubs, and other types of nonprofit agencies. Lacking accurate information, this amount is estimated to be 2 percent of aggregate tuition and fees for years up to 1960, then declining to 1 percent by 1970, reflecting the assumed effect of increased federal and state funding for student aid.

While there are some gaps in the data, the total student-aid estimates in Table A-14 are probably correct within a 5 to 10 percent margin of error and more accurately reflect the level of student assistance than any other source we have come across.

Detailed breakdowns of veterans' benefits are difficult to find. Ordinarily, benefits paid to college students and to veterans in vocational and rehabilitation programs have been reported jointly, and the fraction of the total that has gone to students enrolled in institutions of higher education has changed from year to year. We are indebted to the Veterans Administration for providing the data in Table A-15.

The form of presenting the consolidated institutional accounts shown here, we believe, is useful and relevant to the question of who pays for higher education, and the O'Neill studies for the Commission have provided a consistent reporting base for the 40-year period since 1929–30.

Tables

TABLE A-1
Aggregated institutional income accounts for higher education, 1929-30 (in millions of dollars)

	Public institutions	Private institutions	Total
State			
Local			
Federal	164.2	7.2	171.4
Research and service			
Other			
Tuition and fees	32.5	111.6	144.1
Endowment	6.3	62.3	68.6
Gifts	2.7	23.4	26.1
Sale of services			
Related	14.5	15.8	30.3
Student-aid income			
Public sources	1.0*		1.0
Private sources		3.0*	3.0
Auxiliary enterprises	40.0	70.0	110.0
Total institutional funds	261.2	293.3	554.5 (100%)
Less: noneducational income	−55.5	−88.8	−144.3
Total educational funds of institutions	205.7	204.5	410.2 (100%)
Adjustments:			
Student-aid expenditures			
Subsistence			
Total monetary outlays on education			771.1 (100%)
Forgone income (net of student subsistence)			
Total economic cost			898.7 (100%)

*The distribution of Student Aid Income to public and private institutions for the years 1929–30 through 1951–52 has been estimated.

Burden of costs borne by			
Family	Taxpayer	Philanthropy	Other
	171.4		
144.1			
		68.6	
		26.1	
			30.3
	1.0		
		3.0	
102.3			7.7
246.4	172.4	97.7	38.0
(44.4%)	(31.1%)	(17.6%)	(6.9%)
−102.3	−1.0	−3.0	−38.0
144.1	171.4	94.7	
(35.1%)	(41.8%)	(23.1%)	
−13.0	+1.0	+5.9	
367.0			
498.1	172.4	100.6	
(64.6%)	(22.4%)	(13.0%)	
127.6			
625.7	172.4	100.6	
(69.6%)	(19.2%)	(11.2%)	

TABLE A-2
Aggregated
institutional
income accounts
for higher
education,
1939–40 (in
millions of
dollars)

	Public institutions	Private institutions	Total
State	143.5	7.7	151.2
Local	24.2	0.2	24.4
Federal			
Research and service ⎱			
Other ⎰	36.5	2.4	38.9
Tuition and fees	55.0	145.9	200.9
Endowment	6.7	64.6	71.3
Gifts	5.1	35.3	40.4
Sale of services ⎱			
Related ⎰	23.1	16.5	39.6
Student-aid income			
Public sources	1.2*		1.2
Private sources		3.4*	3.4
Auxiliary enterprises	58.9	85.0	143.9
Total institutional funds	354.2	361.0	715.2 (100%)
Less: noneducational income	−83.2	−104.9	−188.1
Total educational funds of institutions	271.0	256.1	527.1 (100%)
Adjustments:			
Student-aid expenditures			
Subsistence			
Total monetary outlays on education			922.5 (100%)
Forgone income (net of student subsistence)			
Total economic cost			1,112.3 (100%)

*The distribution of Student Aid Income to public and private institutions for the years 1929-30 through 1951–52 has been estimated.

Family	Burden of costs borne by		Other
	Taxpayer	*Philanthropy*	
	151.2		
	24.4		
	38.9		
200.9			
		71.3	
		40.4	
			39.6
	1.2		
		3.4	
133.8			10.1
334.7	215.7	115.1	49.7
(46.8%)	(30.1%)	(16.1%)	(6.9%)
−133.8	−1.2	−3.4	−49.7
200.9	214.5	111.7	
(38.1%)	(40.7%)	(21.2%)	
−22.4	+1.2	+7.4	
409.2			
587.7	215.7	119.1	
(63.7%)	(23.4%)	(12.9%)	
+189.8			
777.5	215.7	119.1	
(69.9%)	(19.4%)	(10.7%)	

TABLE A-3
Aggregated institutional income accounts for higher education, 1949–50 (in millions of dollars)

	Public institutions	Private institutions	Total
State	463.9	27.7	491.6
Local	60.4	1.3	61.7
Federal			
Research and service	70.0*	90.0*	160.0*
Other	176.1	188.3	364.4
Tuition and fees	102.2	292.4	394.6†
Endowment	8.8	87.5	96.3†
Gifts	19.4	99.3	118.7
Sale of services } Related	86.6	73.6	160.2
Student-aid income			
Public sources	4.9‡		4.9
Private sources		11.4‡	11.4
Auxiliary enterprises	246.8	264.5	511.3
Total institutional funds	1,239.1	1,136.0	2,375.1 (100%)
Less: noneducational services	−390.8	−417.0	−807.8
Total educational funds of institutions	848.3	719.0	1,567.3 (100%)
Adjustments:			
Student-aid expenditures			
Subsistence			
Total monetary outlays on education			2,782.0 (100%)
Forgone income (net of student subsistence)			
Total economic cost			4,617.5 (100%)

*Total Federal Funds for research and their distribution to public and private institutions for 1949–50 have been estimated.

†$307.3 million of Other Federal Funds were paid directly to institutions by the Veterans Administration in lieu of veterans' tuition and fees.

‡The distribution of Student Aid Income to public and private institutions for the years 1929–30 through 1951–52 have been estimated.

| | Burden of costs borne by | | |
Family	Taxpayer	Philanthropy	Other
	491.6		
	61.7		
	160.0		
	364.4		
394.6			
		96.3	
		118.7	
			160.2
	4.9		
		11.4	
475.5			35.8
870.1	1,082.6	226.4	196.0
(36.6%)	(45.6%)	(9.5%)	(8.3%)
−475.5	−124.9	−11.4	−196.0
394.6	957.7	215.0	
(25.2%)	(61.1%)	(13.7%)	
−1,054.3	+998.0	+19.3	
1,251.7			
592.0	1,955.7	234.3	
(21.3%)	(70.3%)	(8.4%)	
1,835.5			
2,427.5	1,955.7	234.3	
(52.6%)	(42.3%)	(5.1%)	

TABLE A-4
*Aggregated
institutional
income accounts
for higher
education,
1951–52 (in
millions of
dollars)*

	Public institutions	*Private institutions*	*Total*
State	575.7	35.6	611.3
Local	70.6	1.4	72.0
Federal			
Research and service	91.6	129.2	220.8
Other	129.4	100.8	230.2
Tuition and fees	116.2	330.4	446.6
Endowment	12.1	100.8	112.9
Gifts	26.2	123.6	149.8
Sale of services } *Related*	101.6	87.0	188.6
Student-aid income			
Public sources	6.4*		6.4
Private sources		14.3*	14.3
Auxiliary enterprises	245.6	264.0	509.6
Total institutional funds	1,375.4	1,187.1	2,562.5 (100%)
Less: noneducational services	−422.3	−462.2	−884.5
Total educational funds of institutions	953.1	724.9	1,678.0 (100%)
Adjustments:			
Student-aid expenditures			
Subsistence			
Total monetary outlays on education			2,812.9 (100%)
Forgone income (net of student subsistence)			
Total economic cost			4,810.5 (100%)

*The distribution of Student Aid Income to public and private institutions for the years 1929–30 through 1951–52 has been estimated.

| | Burden of costs borne by | | |
Family	Taxpayer	Philanthropy	Other
	611.3		
	72.0		
	220.8		
	230.2		
446.6			
		112.9	
		149.8	
			188.6
	6.4		
		14.3	
473.9	————	————	35.7
920.5	1,140.7	277.0	224.3
(35.9%)	(44.5%)	(10.8%)	(8.8%)
−473.9	−172.0	−14.3	−224.3
446.6	968.7	262.7	
(26.6%)	(57.7%)	(15.7%)	
−434.9	+372.2	+23.2	
1,174.4	————	————	
1,186.1	1,340.9	285.9	
(42.2%)	(47.7%)	(10.2%)	
1,997.6	————	————	
3,183.7	1,340.9	285.9	
(66.2%)	(27.9%)	(5.9%)	

	Public institutions	Private institutions	Total
State	729.7	21.9	751.6
Local	86.4	1.8	88.2
Federal			
Research and service	114.2	168.5	282.7
Other	102.8	34.0	136.8
Tuition and fees	148.1	406.1	554.2
Endowment	14.7	112.8	127.5
Gifts	38.6	152.7	191.3
Sale of services *Related*	120.4	103.9	224.3
Student-aid income			
Public sources	2.3	0.2	2.5
Private sources	8.0	22.4	30.4
Auxiliary enterprises	286.3	290.6	576.9
Total institutional funds	1,651.5	1,314.9	2,966.4 (100%)
Less: noneducational services	−502.6	−543.5	−1,046.1
Total educational funds of institutions	1,148.9	771.4	1,920.3 (100%)
Adjustments:			
Student-aid expenditures			
Subsistence			
Total monetary outlays on education			3,103.3 (100%)
Forgone income (net of student subsistence)			
Total economic cost			5,342.7 (100%)

	Burden of costs borne by		
Family	*Taxpayer*	*Philanthropy*	*Other*
	751.6		
	88.2		
	282.7		
	136.8		
554.2			
		127.5	
		191.3	
			224.3
	2.5		
		30.4	
536.5	_____	_____	40.4
1,090.7	1,261.8	349.2	264.7
(36.8%)	(42.5%)	(11.8%)	(8.9%)
−536.5	−214.5	−30.4	−264.7
554.2	1,047.3	318.8	
(28.9%)	(54.5%)	(16.6%)	
−337.6	+254.3	+41.5	
1,224.8	_____	_____	
1,441.4	1,301.6	360.3	
(46.4%)	(41.9%)	(11.6%)	
2,269.4	_____	_____	
3,680.8	1,301.6	360.3	
(68.9%)	(24.4%)	(6.7%)	

TABLE A-6
Aggregated institutional income accounts for higher education, 1955–56 (in millions of dollars)

	Public institutions	Private institutions	Total
State	865.1	26.5	891.6
Local	104.0	2.9	106.9
Federal			
Research and service	149.9	205.7	355.6
Other	117.5	20.8	138.3
Tuition and fees	203.0	522.9	725.9
Endowment	16.3	128.8	145.1
Gifts	48.5	197.1	245.6
Sale of services } Related }	145.2	127.7	272.9
Student-aid income			
Public sources	13.5	0.5	14.0
Private sources	10.5	28.5	39.0
Auxiliary enterprises	357.3	336.6	693.9
Total institutional funds	2,030.8	1,598.0	3,628.8 (100%)
Less: noneducational services	−638.9	−647.6	−1,286.5
Total educational funds of institutions	1,381.9	950.4	2,342.3 (100%)
Adjustments:			
Student-aid expenditures			
Subsistence			
Total monetary outlays on education			3,742.3 (100%)
Forgone income (net of student subsistence)			
Total economic cost			6,698.1 (100%)

	Burden of costs borne by		
Family	*Taxpayer*	*Philanthropy*	*Other*
	891.6		
	106.9		
	355.6		
	138.3		
725.9			
		145.1	
		245.6	
			272.9
	14.0		
		39.0	
645.3			48.6
1,371.2	1,506.4	429.7	321.5
(37.8%)	(41.5%)	(11.8%)	(8.9%)
−645.3	−280.7	−39.0	−321.5
725.9	1,225.7	390.7	
(31.0%)	(52.3%)	(16.7%)	
−547.8	+451.1	+53.5	
1,443.2			
1,621.3	1,676.8	444.2	
(43.3%)	(44.8%)	(11.9%)	
2,955.8			
4,577.1	1,676.8	444.2	
(68.4%)	(25.0%)	(6.6%)	

TABLE A-7
Aggregated institutional income accounts for higher education, 1957–58 (in millions of dollars)

	Public institutions	Private institutions	Total
State	1,128.9	27.6	1,156.5
Local	125.8	3.5	129.3
Federal			
Research and service	232.8	301.6	534.4
Other	159.7	18.3	178.0
Tuition and fees	274.2	664.9	939.1
Endowment	15.9	165.8	181.7
Gifts	68.8	256.2	325.0
Sale of services	30.9	16.6	47.5
Related	137.1	133.9	271.0
Student-aid income			
Public sources	17.3	2.8	20.1
Private sources	16.1	35.3	51.4
Auxiliary enterprises	449.0	392.6	841.6
Total institutional funds	2,656.5	2,019.1	4,675.6 (100%)
Less: noneducational services	−825.0	−807.4	−1,632.4
Total educational funds of institutions	1,831.5	1,211.7	3,043.2 (100%)
Adjustments:			
Student-aid expenditures			
Subsistence			
Total monetary outlays on education			4,706.5 (100%)
Forgone income (net of student subsistence)			
Total economic cost			8,247.7 (100%)

	Burden of costs borne by		
Family	*Taxpayer*	*Philanthropy*	*Other*
	1,156.5		
	129.3		
	534.4		
	178.0		
939.1			
		181.7	
		325.0	
			47.5
			271.0
	20.1		
		51.4	
782.7			58.9
1,721.8	2,018.3	558.1	377.4
(36.8%)	(43.2%)	(11.9%)	(8.1%)
−782.7	−420.9	−51.4	−377.4
939.1	1,597.4	506.7	
(30.8%)	(52.5%)	(16.7%)	
−581.5	+451.5	+70.2	
1,723.1			
2,080.7	2,048.9	576.9	
(44.2%)	(43.5%)	(12.3%)	
3,541.2			
5,621.9	2,048.9	576.9	
(68.2%)	(24.8%)	(7.0%)	

	Public institutions	Private institutions	Total
TABLE A-8 *Aggregated institutional income accounts for higher education, 1959–60 (in millions of dollars)*			
State	1,353.1	36.1	1,389.2
Local	147.3	4.5	151.8
Federal			
Research and service	363.5	465.2	828.7
Other	182.9	29.3	212.2
Tuition and fees	332.0	829.8	1,161.8
Endowment	19.7	187.0	206.7
Gifts	85.5	297.7	383.2
Sale of services	37.4	8.0	45.4
Related	168.4	165.3	333.7
Student-aid income			
Public sources	21.5	4.9	26.4
Private sources	20.4	47.5	67.9
Auxiliary enterprises	545.0	461.0	1,006.0
Total institutional funds	3,276.7	2,536.3	5,813.0 (100%)
Less: noneducational services	−1,065.3	−1,035.6	−2,100.9
Total educational funds of institutions	2,211.4	1,500.7	3,712.1 (100%)
Adjustments:			
Student-aid expenditures			
Subsistence			
Total monetary outlays on education			5,567.5 (100%)
Forgone income (net of student subsistence)			
Total economic cost			9,798.5 (100%)

| | Burden of costs borne by | | |
Family	Taxpayer	Philanthropy	Other
	1,389.2		
	151.8		
	828.7		
	212.2		
1,161.8			
		206.7	
		383.2	
			45.4
			333.7
	26.4		
		67.9	
935.6	————	————	70.4
2,097.4 (36.1%)	2,608.3 (44.9%)	657.8 (11.3%)	449.5 (7.7%)
−935.6	−647.9	−67.9	−449.5
1,161.8 (31.3%)	1,960.4 (52.8%)	589.9 (15.9%)	
−445.4	+270.8	+77.9	
+1,952.1	————	————	
2,668.5 (47.9%)	2,231.2 (40.1%)	667.8 (12.0%)	
4,498.2	————	————	
7,166.7 (73.2%)	1,964.0 (20.0%)	667.8 (6.8%)	

TABLE A-9
*Aggregated
institutional
income accounts
for higher
education,
1961–62 (in
millions of
dollars)*

	Public institutions	Private institutions	Total
State	1,640.6	48.5	1,689.1
Local	184.2	7.0	191.2
Federal			
Research and service	548.0	726.4	1,274.4
Other	223.0	44.7	267.7
Tuition and fees	429.7	1,075.6	1,505.3
Endowment	22.6	209.7	232.3
Gifts	98.4	352.3	450.7
Sale of services	40.7	11.7	52.4
Related	209.5	199.6	409.1
Student-aid income			
Public sources	27.8	6.6	34.4
Private sources	25.5	60.4	85.9
Auxiliary enterprises	697.4	576.6	1,274.0
Total institutional funds	4,147.4	3,319.1	7,466.5 (100%)
Less: noneducational services	−1,411.9	−1,399.7	−2,811.6
Total educational funds of institutions	2,735.5	1,919.4	4,654.9 (100%)
Adjustments:			
Student-aid expenditures			
Subsistence			
Total monetary outlays on education			6,888.9 (100%)
Forgone income (net of student subsistence)			
Total economic cost			12,240.6 (100%)

| | Burden of costs borne by | | |
Family	Taxpayer	Philanthropy	Other
	1,689.1		
	191.2		
	1,274.4		
	267.7		
1,505.3			
		232.3	
		450.7	
			52.4
			409.1
	34.4		
		85.9	
1,184.8	____	____	89.2
2,690.1	3,456.8	768.9	550 7
(36.0%)	(46.3%)	(10.3%)	(7.3%)
−1,184.8	−990.2	−85.9	−550.7
1,505.3	2,466.6	683.0	
(32.3%)	(52.9%)	(14.6%)	
−368.3	+144.3	+113.0	
2,345.0	____	____	
3,482.0	2,610.9	796.0	
(50.5%)	(37.9%)	(11.6%)	
5,351.7	____	____	
8,833.7	2,610.9	796.0	
(72.2%)	(21.3%)	(6.5%)	

TABLE A-10
Aggregated institutional income accounts for higher education, 1963–64 (in millions of dollars)

	Public institutions	Private institutions	Total
State	2,077.7	55.9	2,133.6
Local	230.4	10.0	240.4
Federal			
Research and service	754.5	1,042.6	1,797.1
Other	299.3	74.4	373.7
Tuition and fees	582.9	1,316.6	1,899.5
Endowment	27.4	238.8	266.2
Gifts	113.9	437.7	551.6
Sale of services	50.0	15.0	65.0
Related	260.7	242.3	503.0
Student-aid income			
Public sources	35.9	14.2	50.1
Private sources	29.5	71.2	100.7
Auxiliary enterprises	906.4	704.1	1,610.5
Total institutional funds	5,368.7	4,222.7	9,591.4 (100%)
Less: noneducational services	−1,848.3	−1,828.8	−3,677.1
Total educational funds of institutions	3,520.4	2,393.9	5,914.3 (100%)
Adjustments:			
Student-aid expenditures			
Subsistence			
Total monetary outlays on education			8,511.3 (100%)
Forgone income (net of student subsistence)			
Total economic cost			15,386.5 (100%)

| | Burden of costs borne by | | |
Family	Taxpayer	Philanthropy	Other
	2,133.6		
	240.4		
	1,797.1		
	373.7		
1,899.5			
		266.2	
		551.6	
			65.0
			503.0
	50.1		
		100.7	
1,497.8	⎯⎯⎯	⎯⎯⎯	112.7
3,397.3	4,594.9	918.5	680.7
(35.4%)	(47.9%)	(9.6%)	(7.1%)
−1,497.8	−1,397.9	−100.7	−680.7
1,899.5	3,197.0	817.8	
(32.1%)	(54.1%)	(13 8%)	
−402.9	+119.2	+131.1	
2,749.6	⎯⎯⎯	⎯⎯⎯	
4,246.2	3,316.2	948.9	
(49.9%)	(40.0%)	(11.1%)	
6,875.2	⎯⎯⎯	⎯⎯⎯	
11,121.4	3,316.2	948.9	
(72.4%)	(21.5%)	(6.2%)	

	Public institutions	Private institutions	Total
State	2,946.7	85.2	3,031.9
Local	310.8	7.4	318.2
Federal			
Research and service	894.8	1,142.9	2,037.7
Other	480.4	153.8	634.2
Tuition and fees	864.0	1,835.7	2,699.7
Endowment	30.2	288.3	318.5
Gifts	159.8	491.4	651.2
Sale of services ⎫			
Related ⎭	409.3	329.2	738.5
Student-aid income			
Public sources	80.6	39.9	120.5
Private sources	41.7	100.1	141.8
Auxiliary enterprises	1,179.4	924.6	2,104.0
Total institutional funds	7,397.7	5,398.5	12,796.2 (100%)
Less: noneducational services	−2,382.1	−2,251.0	−4,633.1
Total educational funds of institutions	5,015.6	3,147.5	8,163.1 (100%)
Adjustments:			
Student-aid expenditures			
Subsistence			
Total monetary outlays on education			11,582.8 (100%)
Forgone income (net of student subsistence)			
Total economic cost			20,877.3 (100%)

TABLE A-11 *Aggregated institutional income accounts for higher education, 1965–66 (in millions of dollars)*

| | Burden of costs borne by | | |
Family	Taxpayer	Philanthropy	Other
	3,031.9		
	318.2		
	2,037.7		
	634.2		
2,699.7			
		318.5	
		651.2	
			738.5
	120.5		
		141.8	
1,956.7			147.3
4,656.4	6,142.5	1,111.5	885.8
(36.4%)	(48.0%)	(8.7%)	(6.9%)
−1,956.7	−1,648.8	−141.8	−885.8
2,699.7	4,493.7	969.7	
(33.1%)	(55.0%)	(11.9%)	
−746.0	+399.5	+179.6	
3,586.6			
5,540.3	4,893.2	1,149.3	
(47.8%)	(42.2%)	(9.9%)	
9,294.5			
14,834.8	4,893.2	1,149.3	
(71.1%)	(23.4%)	(5.5%)	

TABLE A-12
*Aggregated
institutional
income accounts
for higher
education,
1967–1968 (in
millions of
dollars)*

	Public institutions	Private institutions	Total
State	4,153.4	66.2	4,219.6
Local	482.6	21.1	503.7
Federal			
Research and service	1,120.3	1,263.0	2,383.3
Other	733.2	246.3	979.5
Tuition and fees	1,209.3	2,184.3	3,393.6
Endowment	35.8	328.2	364.0
Gifts	217.1	633.7	850.8
Sale of services	91.8	27.1	118.9
Related	663.2	442.6	1,105.8
Student-aid income			
Public sources	208.8	121.2	330.0
Private sources	54.8	119.1	173.9
Auxiliary enterprises	1,441.4	1,045.3	2,486.7
Total institutional funds	10,412.7	6,498.1	16,910.8 (100%)
Less: noneducational services	−3,300.2	−2,702.6	−6,002.8
Total educational funds of institutions	7,112.5	3,795.5	10,906.9 (100%)
Adjustments:			
Student-aid expenditures			
Subsistence			
Total monetary outlays on education			15,133.6 (100%)
Forgone income (net of student subsistence)			
Total economic cost			27,353.6 (100%)

	Burden of costs borne by		
Family	*Taxpayer*	*Philanthropy*	*Other*
	4,219.6		
	503.7		
	2,383.3		
	979.5		
3,393.6			
		364.0	
		850.8	
			118.9
			1,105.8
	330.0		
		173.9	
2,312.6			174.1
5,706.2	8,416.1	1,388.7	1,398.8
(33.7%)	(49.8%)	(8.2%)	(8.3%)
−2,312.6	−2,117.5	−173.9	−1,398.8
3,393.6	6,298.5	1,214.8	
(31.1%)	(57.8%)	(11.1%)	
−1,519.3	+1,089.9	+214.6	
4,441.5			
6,315.8	7,388.4	1,429.4	
(41.7%)	(48.8%)	(9.4%)	
12,219.9			
18,535.7	7,388.5	1,429.4	
(67.8%)	(27.0%)	(5.2%)	

TABLE A-13
Aggregated
institutional
income accounts
for higher
education,
1969–70 (in
millions of
dollars)

	Public institutions	Private institutions	Total
State	5,850.0	100.0	5,950.0
Local	730.0	40.0	770.0
Federal			
Research and service	1,090.0	1,180.0	2,270.0
Other	1,030.0	340.0	1,370.0
Tuition and fees	1,640.0	2,690.0	4,330.0
Endowment	50.0	400.0	450.0
Gifts	360.0	700.0	1,060.0
Sale of services	100.0	30.0	130.0
Related	1,050.0	820.0	1,870.0
Student-aid income			
Public sources	300.0	170.0	470.0
Private sources	80.0	150.0	230.0
Auxiliary enterprises	1,770.0	1,280.0	3,050.0
Total institutional funds	14,050.0	7,900.0	21,950.0 (100%)
Less: noneducational services	−4,117.5	−3,335.0	−7,452.5
Total educational funds of institutions	9,932.5	4,565.0	14,497.5 (100%)
Adjustments:			
Student-aid expenditures			
Subsistence			
Total monetary outlays on education			19,901.7 (100%)
Forgone income (net of student subsistence)			
Total economic cost			35,643.2 (100%)

| | Burden of costs borne by | | |
Family	Taxpayer	Philanthropy	Other
	5,950.0		
	770.0		
	2,270.0		
	1,370.0		
4,330.0			
		450.0	
		1,060.0	
			130.0
			1,870.0
	470.0		
		230.0	
2,836.5			213.5
7,166.5	10,830.0	1,740.0	2,213.5
(32.6%)	(49.3%)	(7.9%)	(10.1%)
−2,836.5	−2,172.5	−230.0	−2,213.5
4,330.0	8,657.5	1,510.0	
(29.9%)	(59.7%)	(10.4%)	
−2,309.4	+1,736.1	+273.3	
5,704.2			
7,724.8	10,393.6	1,783.3	
(38.8%)	(52.2%)	(9.0%)	
15,741.5			
23,466.3	10,393.6	1,783.3	
(65.8%)	(29.2%)	(5.0%)	

TABLE A-14 *Estimated student aid expenditures (in millions of dollars)*

Year	Veterans benefits (1)	Social security dependents benefits (2)	State scholarship programs (3)	Institutional expenditure from		Current funds (6)	Direct private aid (7)	Total (8)
				Public sources (4)	Private sources (5)			
1929–30				4.0		6.1	2.9	13.0
1939–40				4.6		13.8	4.0	22.4
1949–50	993.1			16.3		37.0	7.9	1,054.3
1951–52	365.8			20.7		39.6	8.9	434.9
1953–54	251.8			2.5	30.4	41.8	11.1	337.6
1955–56	432.1		5.0	14.0	39.0	43.2	14.5	547.8
1957–58	421.4		10.0	20.1	51.4	59.8	18.8	581.5
1959–60	233.1		15.0	26.4	67.9	79.8	23.2	445.4
1961–62	82.9		27.0	34.4	85.9	111.0	27.1	368.3
1963–64	25.1		44.0	50.1	100.7	152.6	30.4	402.9
1965–66		207.0	72.0	120.5	141.8	166.9	37.8	746.0
1967–68	334.9	305.0	120.0	330.0	173.9	214.8	40.7	1,519.3
1969–70	665.1	401.0	200.0	470.0	230.0	300.0	43.3	2,309.4
1970–71	1,117.3	455.0	236.0	575.0	273.0	380.0	48.0	3,084.3

SOURCES OF ESTIMATES:

(1) As provided to the Commission by the Veterans Administration. See Table A-15.

(2) See Table 23, p. 68.

(3) Estimates for most recent years based on surveys conducted by Joseph D. Boyd, executive director of the Illinois State Scholarship Commission; earlier years estimated by Commission staff.

(4) and (5) O'Neill (1973).

(6) O'Neill (1973) and Carnegie Commission staff estimates based on preliminary Office of Education reports for 1969–70 and 1970–71.

(7) Commission staff estimate.

Fiscal year	IHL trainees	Direct benefits cost
1949	1,232,368	$1,099,831,767
1950	1,055,622	993,127,423
1951	731,672	661,277,017
1952	478,492	365,786,825
1953	378,967	248,800,676
1954	423,700	251,760,998
1955	547,612	343,622,957
1956	637,113	432,135,301
1957	644,644	454,951,686
1958	590,267	421,422,095
1959	493,028	347,803,677
1960	331,648	233,107,000
1961	209,973	145,500,000
1962	122,686	82,900,000
1963	68,655	44,800,000
1964	36,109	25,130,000
1965	16,307	8,740,000
1966		
1967	338,785	215,900,000
1968	413,714	334,900,000
1969	528,515	431,700,000
1970	677,240	665,100,000
1971	917,389	1,117,300,000
1972	1,064,513	1,312,500,000

TABLE A-15
Estimate of college-level trainees and their direct benefits cost under the GI bills from 1948–49 through 1971–72*

*Does not include persons under the Dependents Educational Assistance Program or service disabled veterans under the Vocational Rehabilitation Program.

SOURCE: Prepared for the Commission by the Veterans Administration, February 8, 1973.

Appendix B: University Research Activities

In the institutional accounts (Table 4 and Appendix A), we have treated federally sponsored research as though three-fourths of the income received by institutions was for research and development services that could have been performed by noneducational agencies. We have thus eliminated 75 percent of this income from the measures of educational costs. The determination of one-fourth of federal research funds as support of education is meant to imply only that, had such funds from external sources not been present, approximately this magnitude of funds would have been necessary from other sources to provide equivalent educational services. Sponsored research activities perform a dual function, serving both the education of students (most particularly graduate and advanced professional students) and the interests of sponsoring agencies; teaching and research are frequently "joint products" that cannot be separated meaningfully by accounting practices. The 25/75 percent division is somewhat arbitrary, but more accurately reflects true educational cost than would the entire inclusion or exclusion of these federal funds.

It seems likely that, on balance, research and development funds expended by universities produce social benefits considerably in excess of their cost. University researchers, doctors, and engineers—and their institutions—seldom are able to appropriate for private or institutional gain the full monetary value of benefits resulting from the performance of the research function. Strictly applied research yields greater potential for the direct appropriation of benefits (e.g., by use of patents and copyrights), but basic research in areas of new knowledge more commonly produces benefits that are so widely diffused that it is impossible to measure—much less assign property rights to—its results. Nerlove has stated the case succinctly:

> Clearly, it is in the public interest to subsidize collectively the acquisition of new knowledge, especially that of a fundamental or basic character. To some degree, private philanthropy may fill the gap between what individuals would do for their own satisfaction and what would be socially optimal, but such an exact coincidence of public and private interests would be fortuitous. Indeed, the benefits of basic research to society may be so great and so uncertain in character and extent that reliance on individuals' maximizing their own satisfactions may be exceedingly undesirable from a social point of view.[1]

Federally sponsored research in higher education has grown enormously since World War II. As Chart B-1 indicates, the most rapid period of growth was from 1959 to 1968, after which time federal R&D funds expended through universities has declined in real terms. Some of the financial difficulty of major universities over the last several years is attributable to the contraction in federal R&D spending since 1968, particularly in the nonhealth fields in 1971 and 1972.

It is reasonable to assume that, on the average, the societal benefits of research activities by universities outweigh their public and private costs—some persons might argue that these social benefits are sufficient by themselves to justify the major portion of the public subsidy of university education. There is a complementarity between research and teaching activities at the graduate and professional school level (and, to a lesser extent, undergraduate levels) such that each activity enhances the other, and each tends to reduce the cost of the other by contrast with what either would cost in isolation. About two-thirds of direct federal support of institutional activities accrue to the university sector, and this investment of public funds is the major source of support for university research endeavors, which often result in scientific and technological advances and other less measurable forms of new knowledge.

The exclusion of the bulk of research activities from the analysis in this report was intended only to help focus attention on

---

[1]Marc Nerlove, "On Tuition and the Costs of Higher Education: Prolegomena to a Conceptual Framework," *Journal of Political Economy,* vol. 80, p. S203, May–June 1972.

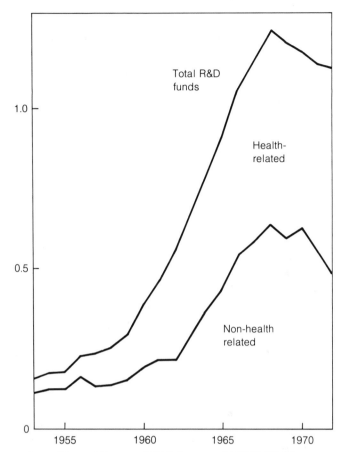

SOURCE: "National Patterns of R & D Resources," NSF 72-300; "Resources for Medical Research," Report No. 12 (1968, updated by N. I. H. staff).

the financing of educational programs. In the long-term development of a society and its economy it may well be that scholarly and research pursuits are of even greater importance than the proportion of a nation's youth who pursue postsecondary education. Fortunately this is not an either/or choice, although societies must always make determinations at the margin whether additional resources devoted to one activity or the other produce greater public benefits.

The Commission has urged that federal support of university research expand at the same annual rate of growth as the gross national product (*Quality and Equality: Revised Recommendations*, 1970c). Such stability and modest growth are necessary if universities are to effectively perform their role in the advancement of knowledge. Reductions in federal support over the last four years, in real terms, as indicated in Chart B-1, have placed federal research and development funding of universities between 20 and 25 percent below this rate of growth in 1973. A significant share of the financial difficulties faced by universities today is attributable to this reversal in federal funding.

Appendix C: The Family Contribution to College Costs: 1971–72 Survey of California Students

Table 11 gave an approximation of the share of total monetary outlays on higher education paid by students and their families, by family income quartile. The average family contribution of 37 percent was determined from Table 4 for the aggregate institutional income account.

The most comprehensive recent survey of how college costs are met was conducted by the California State Scholarship and Loan Commission in 1971. The survey included an approximate 25 percent sample of students attending the University of California campuses, the State University (formerly the State College) campuses, the community colleges, and the independent colleges and universities in the state. Table C-1 summarizes the outlays for college attendance made by students and their parents by income group.

Table C-1 shows the combined family contribution (from parents, student earnings and savings, and loans) toward the cost of attending college in the four higher education sectors in 1971–72. It is noteworthy that the family contribution, even for students in the lowest-income group, was substantial. The lowest-income families contributed about two-thirds of the amount spent by those in the highest-income group.

Table C-2 gives a more detailed breakdown of the share of costs met by parents, students (from term-time and summer earnings, plus personal savings), student loans, and grants and government benefit payments. The student share is surprisingly constant throughout all income ranges. As expected, the parent contribution varied directly with income, and loans and grants varied inversely with family income.

If the California pattern is reasonably typical of family contributions nationwide, then the indirect subsidy could be ap-

TABLE C-1 *Family contribution to the costs of attending California colleges and universities by family income and educational sector, 1971–72*

Family income group	University of California	State University	Community colleges	Independent colleges and universities	Weighted average
			Students attending		
Under $6,000	$1,930	$1,320	$ 970	$1,920	$1,475
$6,000–$9,000	1,950	1,480	1,170	2,280	1,638
$9,000–$12,000	2,120	1,580	1,210	2,460	1,757
$12,000–$15,000	2,250	1,630	1,270	2,710	1,884
$15,000–$18,000	2,360	1,630	1,370	2,720	1,946
Over $18,000	2,530	1,860	1,450	3,310	2,207
Average family contribution	2,190	1,583	1,240	2,575	1,817
Average grant or benefit received	520	257	210	785	410
Total student resources	$2,710	$1,840	$1,450	$3,360	$2,227

SOURCE: California State Scholarship and Loan Commission Report #1, Student Financial Aid Research Series, Tables 13–16, Appendix IV, were used for this summary, as corrected by CSSLC to take account of term-time student earnings omitted in the tables in the text of their report.

TABLE C-2 *Average student resources for meeting the costs of attending college, California, 1971–72 (in dollars, and percentages of total resources)*

Family income group	Parents	Students	Student loans	Grants and benefits
	Students attending public institutions			
Under $6,000	$163	$1,027	$217	$527
	8.4%	53.2%	11.2%	27.2%
$6,000–$9,000	230	1,123	180	450
	11.6%	56.6%	9.1%	22.7%
$9,000–$12,000	320	1,167	153	333
	16.2%	59.1%	7.8%	16.9%
$12,000–$15,000	427	1,157	133	263
	21.6%	58.4%	6.7%	13.3%
$15,000–$18,000	507	1,170	110	217
	25.3%	58.4%	5.5%	10.8%
Over $18,000	733	1,137	77	177
	34.5%	53.6%	3.6%	8.3%

SOURCE: See Table C-1.

portioned by type of institution to estimate by income group the fraction of total monetary outlays on education contributed by families. From the aggregate higher education income account (Table 4) the indirect subsidy per FTE student in the public and private sectors was as follows for 1970–71:

Private colleges and universities:	
Per capita governmental contribution	$ 432
Per capita philanthropic contribution	716
TOTAL	$1,148
Public colleges and universities:	
Per capita governmental contribution	$1,396
Per capita philanthropic contribution	63
TOTAL	$1,459

Students attending private institutions			
Parents	Students	Student loans	Grants and benefits
$ 340	$1,160	$420	$ 940
11.9%	40.6%	14.7%	32.8%
490	1,290	500	1,060
14.7%	38.6%	15.0%	31.7%
700	1,330	430	920
20.7%	39.4%	12.7%	27.2%
970	1,340	400	790
27.7%	38.3%	11.4%	22.6%
1,220	1,220	330	650
35.7%	35.7%	9.6%	19.0%
1,840	1,260	210	350
50.3%	34.4%	5.7%	9.6%

In their study of higher education finance in California, *Benefits and Costs of Public Higher Education in California* (1969), Hansen and Weisbrod determined the indirect subsidies in the public sector to be approximately $720 in the community colleges, $1,400 in the state colleges, and $1,700 in the University of California. This relationship between subsidy levels appears to be borne out by the experience of other states. Thus it would seem reasonable to assume that, generally, per student subsidies in public two-year colleges are about one-half of the subsidy per student in four-year colleges, and that the subsidies in universities are generally about 25 percent higher than in the four-year colleges. This assumption provides the following estimate of per capita subsidies (from both public and philanthropic sources), by type of institution:

Public two-year colleges	$ 791
Public four-year colleges	1,343
Public universities	1,686
Private colleges and universities	1,091

Table C-3, based on Table C-1 and the above subsidy estimates, indicates the approximate family contribution (parents, students, plus student loans) as a percentage of the total monetary outlay on higher education by family income level and type of institutions for California in 1971–72.[1]

The family contribution ranges from 43.0 percent for the under-$6,000 group up to 61.7 percent for the top income group. These figures are slightly higher than the national averages suggested in Table 10 chiefly because students in the California survey estimated their total living costs while in college, whereas in Table 3 and Appendix A tables subsistence costs include only estimates of room, board, and educationally related incidentals. However, the pattern in Table C-3 is similar

---

[1] The student resources survey was for 1971–72, while the subsidy estimates are based on 1970–71 national data. Given the tight budgetary situation in which the public colleges and universities in California found themselves in the early 1970s, this one-year difference is not likely to have an appreciable effect on the calculations.

TABLE C-3 *Percentage of total monetary outlays on higher education met by family resources, by family income and educational sector, California, 1971–72*

Family income group	Students attending				Weighted average
	University of California	State University	Community colleges	Independent colleges and universities	
Under $6,000	43.8%	41.5%	43.3%	43.1%	43.0%
$6,000–$9,000	44.1	46.5	52.2	51.2	48.3
$9,000–$12,000	48.1	49.7	54.1	55.3	51.3
$12,000–$15,000	51.0	51.2	56.7	60.9	53.7
$15,000–$18,000	53.5	51.2	61.1	61.1	55.8
Over $18,000	57.6	58.5	64.7	74.7	61.7
Weighted average	50.4	50.3	56.2	59.9	53.0

SOURCE: See Table C-1.

to that indicated in Table 10 and confirms the conclusion that the private expenditure necessary to attend college remains substantial for students from low-income families.

Appendix D: Estimated Distribution of Tax Burden and Institutional Subsidies, by Income Group

As we have defined the monetary outlay on higher education—excluding three-fourths of federally sponsored research conducted by universities, but including benefits paid to veterans and dependents under social security enrolled in college (see pp. 23–25)—the taxpayer contribution in 1970–71 was $11,932 million. Of this amount $3,977 million came from federal sources and $7,955 million from state and local governments.

A rough estimate of the distribution of the tax burden was made in Table 14. It was assumed that the $3,977 million federal contribution is borne by income groups as the federal income tax is apportioned. (This is an oversimplification, for the social security tax and excise levies are much less progressive than the federal income tax; on the other hand, the estate tax is probably more progressive in its incidence than is the income tax.) Total adjusted gross incomes, by income group, as reported by the Internal Revenue Service, are shown in column 1 of Table D-1. Since the federal contribution to higher education expense in 1970–71 was 4.746 percent of total income tax revenues, tax liabilities for each income group have been multiplied by that factor.

State and local taxes are assumed to be borne as shown in column 2 of Table 12. Revenues produced by these rates have been multiplied by 18.122 percent to produce the $7,955 million revenue that represents state and local contributions as shown in column 3 of Table D-1. Columns 4 and 5 indicate the estimated combined taxpayer burden.

This method of estimating the higher educational tax burden provides a very rough measure, but the relative contribution by each income group probably would not be changed greatly by more sophisticated techniques.

TABLE D-1 *Estimated distribution of higher education tax burden, by family income group, 1970 (in billions of dollars)*

Family income group	Adjusted gross income	Federal tax contributions	State and local tax contributions	Total	Percentage
Under $3,000	$ 11.6	$ .024	$ .225	$ .249	2.09
$3,000–$5,000	35.6	.143	.529	.672	5.63
$5,000–$7,500	70.6	.307	.934	1.241	10.40
$7,500–$10,000	92.4	.486	1.189	1.675	14.04
$10,000–$15,000	171.6	.977	2.178	3.155	26.44
Over $15,000	228.8	2.040	2.900	4.940	41.40
TOTAL	$634.4	$3.977	$7.955	$11.932	100.00

SOURCE: Computed from U.S. Internal Revenue Service, *Statistics of Income, 1970, Individual Income Tax Returns.*

The public subsidy benefits shown in Table 14 have been allocated based on census and U.S. Office of Education data on college attendance by family income level. Table D-2 shows the number of college attenders among the 18–24 age group by family income, as reported by the U.S. Bureau of the Census for October 1971. The number of attenders in column 1 includes both students currently enrolled, and others not currently enrolled but who have had one or more years of college education. Of the 8,030,000 college attenders reported, approximately 70 percent were currently in college in fall 1971.

TABLE D-2 The distribution of college attenders among family income groups, by type of institution attended (in thousands)

Family income group	Total attenders	Public institutions		
		Universities	Four-year	Two-year
Under $3,000	388	82	121	132
$3,000–$5,000	741	140	207	230
$5,000–$7,500	1,155	210	311	348
$7,500–$10,000	1,415	340	416	334
$10,000–$15,000	2,147	580	623	446
Over $15,000	2,184	775	419	236
TOTAL	8,030	2,127	2,097	1,726

SOURCE: Column 1 computed from "Social and Economic Characteristics of Students, October 1971," U.S. Bureau of the Census, ser. P-20, no. 241, October 1972, Table 14; distribution by type of institutions from unpublished Office of Education data reported by Hartman (1972*b*, p. 493).

The distribution of students among types of institutions is based on unpublished Office of Education data, as reported by Hartman (1972*b*, p. 493).

The total institutional subsidy from tax revenues was $8,789 million in public institutions in 1970–71. Assuming that government funded student-aid benefits were equal per capita in both public and private institutions (a reasonable assumption, since these were predominantly veterans, social security, and state scholarship benefits), an additional $1,766 million must be added. Using the formula described in Appendix C, this implies an average per student subsidy of $2,348 in state universities, $1,878 in public four-year colleges, and $940 in community colleges.[1]

In the private sector, public subsidies totaled $760 million through institutions and $617 million in the form of student aid. Per student subsidies are thus estimated to be $803, $642, and $321 for the private universities, four-year colleges, and two-year colleges, respectively.

Table D-3 shows the resulting estimate of subsidies from tax sources, by family income group.

[1] These amounts are slightly below those indicated in Appendix C by virtue of the inclusion of former (but not currently enrolled) beneficiaries among the 18–24 population. However, this should not significantly alter the distribution among income groups.

| | Private institutions | |
Universities	Four-year	Two-year
9	38	6
32	122	10
55	203	28
75	225	25
125	339	34
216	494	44
512	1,421	147

	Subsidy from tax sources	
Family income group	$ millions	Percentage
Under $3,000	$ 576	4.8%
$3,000–$5,000	1,041	8.7
$5,000–$7,500	1,588	13.3
$7,500–$10,000	2,106	17.7
$10,000–$15,000	3,283	27.5
Over $15,000	3,338	28.0
TOTAL	$11,932	100.0%

TABLE D-3 Estimated distribution of higher educational subsidies from tax sources, 1970–71

Appendix E: Projections for 1983

The recommendations in this report anticipate a gradual increase in the federal share of college funding, but an overall maintenance of the balance between governmental and family contributions.

The size of the 18-to-24-year-old population will increase by 2.1 million, about 16 percent, between 1970 and 1983. We anticipate—if our financing recommendations become practice—an increase in the ratio of total FTE students enrolled to the 18–24 age group population from about 0.26 to 0.31 by 1983 (6.3 million to 9.0 million).

In keeping with our recommendation that increased federal support predominantly be in the form of direct student aid, we project in Table E-1 an increase in student aid funding from $3 billion in 1970–71 (see Table 4) to approximately $8.5 billion by 1983. This implies an increase in per capita student aid from $490 to approximately $950 by 1983.

Table E-1, projecting the aggregate institutional accounts to 1983 (in 1970 constant dollars), also reflects our tuition recommendations. Tuition charges in private colleges and universities are anticipated to increase by 3.25 percent per year in constant dollars (the increase will be more rapid in current dollars reflecting inflationary increases in costs and prices). In the public sector student charges are estimated to rise by 7.2 percent per year in constant dollars, the rate necessary to return the public-private tuition ratio to its average of 20 years ago. If, however, the rate of inflation between 1970 and 1983 equals its average of 2.75 percent recorded during the preceding decade, then the estimated rates of increase in student charges in current dollars would be 10.5 percent in the public sector and 6.0 percent in private institutions. If the rate of inflation continues

TABLE E-1 *The projected account for education for 1983 (in billions of dollars, 1970)*

Income source	Public sector	Private sector	Total	Costs borne by Family	Costs borne by Taxpayers	Costs borne by Philanthropy
State and local government	10.1	0.6	10.7		10.7	
Federal government	2.7	0.8	3.5		3.5	
Tuition and fees	6.6	5.1	11.7	11.7		
Endowment income	0.2	0.6	0.8			0.8
Gifts	0.7	1.1	1.8			1.8
Total educational funds of institutions	20.3	8.2	28.5 (100.0%)	11.7 (41.2%)	14.2 (50.0%)	2.6 (8.8%)
Adjustments						
Subsistence				9 5		
Student aid				−8.5	7.2	0.5
Total monetary outlays on education			37.2 (100.0%)	12.7 (34.1%)	12.4 (57.5%)	3.1 (8.4%)
Forgone income (net of student subsistence)				32.4		
Total economic cost			69.6 (100.0%)	45.1 (64.8%)	21.4 (30.7%)	3.1 (4.5%)

at 2.75 percent, all dollar amounts in Table E-1 should be multiplied by 1.38 to estimate current dollar totals in 1983.

In *The More Effective Use of Resources* we recommended a growth path for higher education that would place total current fund expenditures in higher education at approximately $41.4 billion (in 1970 constant dollars) in 1980–81. Current fund expenditures, however, include all sponsored research, auxiliary enterprise costs, and the cost of services sold to nonstudents and related activities which are not included in educational funds in Table E-1. These items amounted to approximately $9 billion in 1970–71 (compare Tables 3 and 4), and are predicted to grow to nearly $14 billion by 1983. Thus, total current fund expenditures in 1983 would be about $43 billion.

We have projected costs in Table E-1 assuming that 1983 FTE enrollments will be approximately 6.9 million in public institutions and 2.1 million in private colleges and universities.

Most of the student aid funding from taxpayer sources in Table E-1 is assumed to originate under federal programs. Thus, if one adds institutional support and student assistance from federal sources, plus an estimated $3 billion in sponsored research funds omitted in Table E-1, the federal contribution would be about 50 percent of all governmental outlays on higher education.

Appendix F: State Aid for Private Colleges and Universities

State assistance of private institutions has a long history in the United States, although until the last decade it was not a common practice, and the amounts involved were relatively small. In Pennsylvania, state aid has gone to the University of Pennsylvania, a private university, since colonial days, and the state today has several "state-related" and "state-assisted" institutions. After the passage of the Morrill Act in 1861, several states (e.g., New York, Massachusetts), selected private institutions as their land-grant designate. However, broad state programs either to assist students to attend private colleges or in the form of direct institutional aid are a relatively novel feature in American higher education.

In 1972, thirty-one of the states had in effect one or more programs of assistance for private colleges and universities, and several other states were in the process of deliberating such proposals.[1] Twenty-eight states had enacted student-aid programs of scholarships, loans, or tuition grants that enabled state residents to attend private colleges. (Most such programs were limited to attending a private institution within the state.)

In this report we have urged all states to develop state scholarship programs, and have recommended that federal matching monies be made available under the Higher Education Act of 1972. We have also encouraged states to take action to gradually narrow the tuition differential between public and private institutions, including the granting of direct institutional aid to private colleges. At the present time five states have such direct

---

[1] Carol H. Shulman, *State Aid to Private Higher Education*, American Association for Higher Education (1972). The Education Commission of the States reports that four additional states have enacted legislation during the past year.

grant programs in effect (Illinois, Maryland, New York, Oregon, and Pennsylvania), three others have contractual arrangements with private institutions in their state to enable them to enroll additional state residents (Connecticut, Minnesota, and North Carolina), and at least seven others have contracts with one or more private institutions for supporting study in particular fields (predominantly medicine and dentistry). In 1971–72, state appropriations under these direct institutional aid provisions totaled nearly $100 million.

New York ($26.9 million in 1971–72) and Maryland ($1.9 million in 1971–72) have based their programs of private institutional aid on degrees awarded. Except for Pennsylvania's historic support of selected private institutions, New York has had the longest experience with direct aid (since 1968), and awards $400 for each bachelor's and master's degree awarded and $2,400 for each doctorate.[2] Maryland grants $200 per associate degree and $500 per bachelor's degree. At the undergraduate level these grants average less than $100 per year per student enrolled, constituting about 5 percent or less of educational costs at the eligible private institutions.

Illinois ($6 million) and Oregon ($2 million) base their grants on enrollment of state residents in private colleges. Illinois awards $100 per lower-division student and $200 for each upper-division student; and Oregon awards $250 for every 45 quarter-hours completed.

In selected institutions Pennsylvania bases its support on programs of benefit to the state, and has no fixed grant formula. Pittsburgh and Temple receive general funding support as state-related institutions, and the University of Pennsylvania and several others receive amounts determined by the legislature as "state-aided" institutions.

The Commission has recommended that aid to private institutions be based upon enrollment so as to provide greater flexibility in grant formulas, particularly as regards differential treatment for lower- and upper-division education. In view of the external benefits that accrue to society from both public and private colleges, we have encouraged states to assume greater

---

[2] Governor Rockefeller recommended in April 1973 an increase in these amounts to: $300 at the associate level, $800 at the baccalaureate level, $600 for master's degrees, and $3,000 for doctorates.

responsibility for assuring the fiscal health of the private sector. On the other hand, we have cautioned against state assistance that would be greater than one-fifth of the cost of education in a comparable public institution, partly to assure the continued independence of the private institutions and partly to ensure that total subsidies per student (from both public and philanthropic sources) in private colleges do not exceed those made available for students selecting to attend a state college or university.

In 1970–71, for example, the average student attending a private institution paid $1,683 in tuition and fees, and was assisted by subsidies amounting to $1,147 ($432 from governmental sources plus $715 from gifts and endowments). The average student in a public institution paid $416 in tuition and fees and received a subsidy (predominantly from governmental sources) of $2,025.[3] If our suggested one-fifth of public educational cost guideline were applied, a state institutional grant would not exceed $488 per student in private institutions, and the total subsidy received by the average student enrolled in a private college would have been $1,635 in 1970–71, or about 80 percent of the equivalent subsidy from all sources in a public institution.

Except for the uncommon case of Pennsylvania, present state institutional-aid programs are far below our suggested ceiling. If, as we have recommended, over the next 10 to 15 years public tuition charges rise to about one-third of educational costs, the total subsidy per student would become approximately the same in the two sectors—although students in private institutions would still be paying considerably higher tuition than those in public colleges, and the portion of the total student subsidy borne by the taxpayer would be much greater in public institutions.

The Commission recognizes that over the years different states will develop different patterns of student assistance and institutional support, depending upon local traditions and legal and constitutional factors. We have thought it useful, however, to set out a guideline for direct institutional aid in view of the growing interest in, and implementation of, programs to assist private colleges and universities.

---

[3] Aggregate amounts in Table 4 divided by FTE degree-credit enrollments.

References

Becker, G. S.: *Human Capital: A Theoretical and Empirical Analysis, with Special Reference to Education*, National Bureau of Economic Research, New York, 1964.

Bowen, H. R., and P. Servelle: *Who Benefits from Higher Education and Who Should Pay?*, American Association for Higher Education, Washington, D.C., 1972.

California State Scholarship and Loan Commission: *Student Resources Survey*, Sacramento, Calif., 1972.

Carnegie Commission on Higher Education: *A Chance to Learn: An Action Agenda for Equal Opportunity in Higher Education*, McGraw-Hill Book Company, New York, 1970a.

Carnegie Commission on Higher Education: *The Open-Door Colleges: Policies for Community Colleges*, McGraw-Hill Book Company, New York, 1970b.

Carnegie Commission on Higher Education: *Quality and Equality: Revised Recommendations, New Levels of Federal Responsibility for Higher Education*, McGraw-Hill Book Company, New York, 1970c.

Carnegie Commission on Higher Education: *The Capitol and the Campus: State Responsibility for Postsecondary Education*, McGraw-Hill Book Company, New York, 1971a.

Carnegie Commission on Higher Education: *Less Time, More Options: Education beyond the High School*, McGraw-Hill Book Company, New York, 1971b.

Carnegie Commission on Higher Education: *New Students and New Places: Policies for the Future Growth and Development of American Higher Education*, McGraw-Hill Book Company, New York, 1971c.

Carnegie Commission on Higher Education: *The More Effective Use of Resources: An Imperative for Higher Education*, McGraw-Hill Book Company, New York, 1972.

Carnegie Commission on Higher Education: *College Graduates and Jobs: Adjusting to a New Labor Market Situation,* McGraw-Hill Book Company, New York, 1973.

Carter, C. F.: "Costs and Benefits of Mass Higher Education," address before a conference on financing of higher education, University of Lancaster, Lancaster, September 1972. (Mimeographed.)

Cartter, A. M.: "Student Financial Aid," in L. Wilson (ed.), *Universal Higher Education,* American Council on Education, Washington, D.C., 1972.

Cheit, E. F.: *The New Depression in Higher Education: A Study of Financial Conditions at 41 Colleges and Universities,* McGraw-Hill Book Company, New York, 1971.

College Entrance Examination Board: *New Approaches to Student Financial Aid,* Report of the Panel on Financial Need Analysis, New York, 1971.

City University of New York, Office for Research in Higher Education: *The Graduates: A Follow-up Study of New York City High School Graduates of 1970,* New York, 1971.

Denison, E. F.: *The Sources of Economic Growth in the United States and the Alternatives before Us,* Committee for Economic Development, New York, 1962.

Economic Report of the President: Transmitted to the Congress January 1969, Washington, D.C., 1969.

Economic Report of the President: Transmitted to the Congress January 1973, Washington, D.C., 1973.

Friedman, M.: "The Higher Schooling in America," *The Public Interest,* no. 11, pp. 108–112, Spring 1968.

Hansen, W. L., and B. A. Weisbrod: *Benefits, Costs, and Finance of Public Higher Education,* Markham Publishing Company, Chicago, 1969.

Hartman, R. W.: *Credit for College: Public Policy for Student Loans,* McGraw-Hill Book Company, New York, 1971.

Hartman, R. W.: "Equity Implications of State Tuition Policy and Student Loans," in T. W. Schultz (ed.), *Investment in Education: The Equity-Efficiency Quandary,* University of Chicago Press, Chicago, 1972*a*.

Hartman, R. W.: "Higher Education Subsidies: An Analysis of Selected Programs in Current Legislation," in *The Economics of Federal Subsidy Programs,* a compendium of papers submitted to the Joint Economic Committee, U.S. Congress, Washington, D.C., 1972*b*.

Hoenack, S. A.: "The Efficient Allocation of Subsidies to College Students," *American Economic Review*, vol. 61, pp. 302–311, June 1971.

Jellema, W. W.: *Redder and Much Redder: A Follow-up Study to "The Red and the Black,"* Association of American Colleges, Washington, D.C., 1971.

Kendrick, J. W.: *Productivity Trends in the United States*, Princeton University Press, Princeton, N.J., 1961.

Mundel, D. S.: "Federal Aid to Higher Education: An Analysis of Federal Subsidies to Undergraduate Education," in *The Economics of Federal Subsidy Programs*, a compendium of papers submitted to the Joint Economic Committee, U.S. Congress, Washington, D.C., 1972.

O'Neill, June: *Resource Use in Higher Education*, Carnegie Commission on Higher Education, Berkeley, Calif., 1971.

O'Neill, June: *Sources of Funds to Colleges and Universities*, Carnegie Commission on Higher Education, Berkeley, Calif., 1973.

Panel on Educational Innovation, J. R. Zacharias, Chairman: *Educational Opportunity Bank: A Report of the Panel on Educational Innovation to the U.S. Commissioner of Education, the Director of the National Science Foundation, and the Special Assistant to the President for Science and Technology*, Washington, D.C., 1967.

Pechman, Joseph A.: "The Distributional Effects of Public Higher Education in California," *Journal of Human Resources*, vol. 5, pp. 361–370, Summer 1970.

Pechman, Joseph A.: "Note on the Intergenerational Transfer of Public Higher-Education Benefits," in T. W. Schultz (ed.), *Investment in Education: The Equity-Efficiency Quandary*, University of Chicago Press, Chicago, 1972.

Peltzman, S.: "The Effect of Government Subsidies-in-Kind on Private Expenditures: The Case of Higher Education," *Journal of Political Economy*, vol. 18, pp. 1–27, January–February 1973.

Rehn, Gösta: *Prospective View on Patterns of Working Time*, Report No. 1B, Organisation for Economic Cooperation and Development, Paris, 1972.

Schultz, T. W.: *Investment in Human Capital*, The Free Press, New York, 1971.

Schultz, T. W. (ed.): *Investment in Education: The Equity-Efficiency Quandary*, University of Chicago Press, Chicago, 1972.

Solow, R. M.: "Technical Change and the Aggregate Production Function," *Review of Economics and Statistics,* vol. 39, no. 3, pp. 312–320, August 1957.

Taubman, P., and T. Wales: *Education as an Investment and a Screening Device,* unpublished manuscript, National Bureau of Economic Research, New York, 1972.

U.S. Bureau of the Census: "Social and Economic Characteristics of Students: October 1971," *Current Population Reports,* ser. P-20, no. 241, Washington, D.C., 1972.

U.S. Office of Education: *Projections of Educational Statistics to 1975–76, 1966 Edition,* Washington, D.C., 1966.

U.S. Office of Education: *Digest of Educational Statistics, 1971 Edition,* Washington, D.C., 1972a.

U.S. Office of Education: *Projections of Educational Statistics to 1980–81, 1971 Edition,* Washington, D.C., 1972b.

Walters, E. (ed.): *Graduate Education Today,* American Council on Education, Washington, D.C., 1965.

Carnegie Commission on Higher Education
Sponsored Research Studies

THE RISE OF THE ARTS ON THE AMERICAN
CAMPUS
Jack Morrison

THE UNIVERSITY AND THE CITY: EIGHT
CASES OF INVOLVEMENT
*George Nash, Dan Waldorf, and Robert E.
Price*

THE BEGINNING OF THE FUTURE:
A HISTORICAL APPROACH TO GRADUATE
EDUCATION IN THE ARTS AND SCIENCES
Richard J. Storr

ACADEMIC TRANSFORMATION: SEVENTEEN
INSTITUTIONS UNDER PRESSURE
David Riesman and Verne A. Stadtman (eds.)

WHERE COLLEGES ARE AND WHO ATTENDS:
EFFECTS OF ACCESSIBILITY ON COLLEGE
ATTENDANCE
*C. Arnold Anderson, Mary Jean Bowman, and
Vincent Tinto*

NEW DIRECTIONS IN LEGAL EDUCATION
*Herbert L. Packer and Thomas Ehrlich
abridged and unabridged editions*

THE UNIVERSITY AS AN ORGANIZATION
James A. Perkins (ed.)

THE EMERGING TECHNOLOGY:
INSTRUCTIONAL USES OF THE COMPUTER
IN HIGHER EDUCATION
Roger E. Levien

A STATISTICAL PORTRAIT OF HIGHER
EDUCATION
Seymour E. Harris

THE HOME OF SCIENCE:
THE ROLE OF THE UNIVERSITY
Dael Wolfle

EDUCATION AND EVANGELISM:
A PROFILE OF PROTESTANT COLLEGES
C. Robert Pace

PROFESSIONAL EDUCATION:
SOME NEW DIRECTIONS
Edgar H. Schein

THE NONPROFIT RESEARCH INSTITUTE:
ITS ORIGIN, OPERATION, PROBLEMS, AND
PROSPECTS
Harold Orlans

THE INVISIBLE COLLEGES:
A PROFILE OF SMALL, PRIVATE COLLEGES
WITH LIMITED RESOURCES
Alexander W. Astin and Calvin B. T. Lee

AMERICAN HIGHER EDUCATION:
DIRECTIONS OLD AND NEW
Joseph Ben-David

A DEGREE AND WHAT ELSE?
CORRELATES AND CONSEQUENCES OF A
COLLEGE EDUCATION
*Stephen B. Withey, Jo Anne Coble, Gerald
Gurin, John P. Robinson, Burkhard Strumpel,
Elizabeth Keogh Taylor, and Arthur C. Wolfe*

THE MULTICAMPUS UNIVERSITY:
A STUDY OF ACADEMIC GOVERNANCE
Eugene C. Lee and Frank M. Bowen

INSTITUTIONS IN TRANSITION:
A PROFILE OF CHANGE IN HIGHER
EDUCATION
(INCORPORATING THE 1970 STATISTICAL
REPORT)
Harold L. Hodgkinson

EFFICIENCY IN LIBERAL EDUCATION:
A STUDY OF COMPARATIVE INSTRUCTIONAL
COSTS FOR DIFFERENT WAYS OF ORGANIZ-
ING TEACHING-LEARNING IN A LIBERAL
ARTS COLLEGE
Howard R. Bowen and Gordon K. Douglass

CREDIT FOR COLLEGE:
PUBLIC POLICY FOR STUDENT LOANS
Robert W. Hartman

MODELS AND MAVERICKS:
A PROFILE OF PRIVATE LIBERAL ARTS
COLLEGES
Morris T. Keeton

BETWEEN TWO WORLDS:
A PROFILE OF NEGRO HIGHER EDUCATION
Frank Bowles and Frank A. DeCosta

BREAKING THE ACCESS BARRIERS:
A PROFILE OF TWO-YEAR COLLEGES
Leland L. Medsker and Dale Tillery

ANY PERSON, ANY STUDY:
AN ESSAY ON HIGHER EDUCATION IN THE
UNITED STATES
Eric Ashby

THE NEW DEPRESSION IN HIGHER
EDUCATION:
A STUDY OF FINANCIAL CONDITIONS AT 41
COLLEGES AND UNIVERSITIES
Earl F. Cheit

FINANCING MEDICAL EDUCATION:
AN ANALYSIS OF ALTERNATIVE POLICIES
AND MECHANISMS
Rashi Fein and Gerald I. Weber

HIGHER EDUCATION IN NINE COUNTRIES:
A COMPARATIVE STUDY OF COLLEGES AND
UNIVERSITIES ABROAD
*Barbara B. Burn, Philip G. Altbach, Clark Kerr,
and James A. Perkins*

BRIDGES TO UNDERSTANDING:
INTERNATIONAL PROGRAMS OF AMERICAN
COLLEGES AND UNIVERSITIES
Irwin T. Sanders and Jennifer C. Ward

GRADUATE AND PROFESSIONAL EDUCATION,
1980:
A SURVEY OF INSTITUTIONAL PLANS
Lewis B. Mayhew

THE AMERICAN COLLEGE AND AMERICAN
CULTURE:
SOCIALIZATION AS A FUNCTION OF HIGHER
EDUCATION
Oscar Handlin and Mary F. Handlin

RECENT ALUMNI AND HIGHER EDUCATION:
A SURVEY OF COLLEGE GRADUATES
Joe L. Spaeth and Andrew M. Greeley

CHANGE IN EDUCATIONAL POLICY:
SELF-STUDIES IN SELECTED COLLEGES AND
UNIVERSITIES
Dwight R. Ladd

STATE OFFICIALS AND HIGHER EDUCATION:
A SURVEY OF THE OPINIONS AND
EXPECTATIONS OF POLICY MAKERS IN NINE
STATES
Heinz Eulau and Harold Quinley

ACADEMIC DEGREE STRUCTURES:
INNOVATIVE APPROACHES
PRINCIPLES OF REFORM IN DEGREE
STRUCTURES IN THE UNITED STATES
Stephen H. Spurr

COLLEGES OF THE FORGOTTEN AMERICANS:
A PROFILE OF STATE COLLEGES AND
REGIONAL UNIVERSITIES
E. Alden Dunham

FROM BACKWATER TO MAINSTREAM:
A PROFILE OF CATHOLIC HIGHER
EDUCATION
Andrew M. Greeley

THE ECONOMICS OF THE MAJOR PRIVATE
UNIVERSITIES
William G. Bowen
(Out of print, but available from University Microfilms.)

THE FINANCE OF HIGHER EDUCATION
Howard R. Bowen
(Out of print, but available from University Microfilms.)

ALTERNATIVE METHODS OF FEDERAL
FUNDING FOR HIGHER EDUCATION
Ron Wolk
(Out of print, but available from University Microfilms.)

INVENTORY OF CURRENT RESEARCH ON
HIGHER EDUCATION 1968
Dale M. Heckman and Warren Bryan Martin
(Out of print, but available from University Microfilms.)

The following technical reports are available from the Carnegie Commission on Higher Education, 2150 Shattuck Ave., Berkeley, California 94704.

RESOURCE USE IN HIGHER EDUCATION:
TRENDS IN OUTPUT AND INPUTS, 1930–1967
June O'Neill

TRENDS AND PROJECTIONS OF PHYSICIANS
IN THE UNITED STATES 1967–2002
Mark S. Blumberg

MAY 1970:
THE CAMPUS AFTERMATH OF CAMBODIA
AND KENT STATE
Richard E. Peterson and John A. Bilorusky

MENTAL ABILITY AND HIGHER EDUCATIONAL
ATTAINMENT IN THE 20TH CENTURY
Paul Taubman and Terence Wales

AMERICAN COLLEGE AND UNIVERSITY
ENROLLMENT TRENDS IN 1971
Richard E. Peterson

PAPERS ON EFFICIENCY IN THE
MANAGEMENT OF HIGHER EDUCATION
Alexander M. Mood, Colin Bell, Lawrence
Bogard, Helen Brownlee, and Joseph McCloskey

AN INVENTORY OF ACADEMIC INNOVATION
AND REFORM
Ann Heiss

ESTIMATING THE RETURNS TO EDUCATION:
A DISAGGREGATED APPROACH
Richard S. Eckaus

SOURCES OF FUNDS TO COLLEGES AND
UNIVERSITIES
June O'Neill

NEW DEPRESSION IN HIGHER
EDUCATION—TWO YEARS LATER
Earl F. Cheit

The following reprints are available from the Carnegie Commission on Higher Education, 2150 Shattuck Ave., Berkeley, California 94704.

ACCELERATED PROGRAMS OF MEDICAL EDUCATION, *by Mark S. Blumberg, reprinted from* JOURNAL OF MEDICAL EDUCATION, *vol. 46, no. 8, August 1971.**

*The Commission's stock of this reprint has been exhausted.

SCIENTIFIC MANPOWER FOR 1970–1985, by Allan M. Cartter, reprinted from SCIENCE, vol. 172, no. 3979, pp. 132–140, April 9, 1971.

A NEW METHOD OF MEASURING STATES' HIGHER EDUCATION BURDEN, by Neil Timm, reprinted from THE JOURNAL OF HIGHER EDUCATION, vol. 42, no. 1, pp. 27–33, January 1971.*

REGENT WATCHING, by Earl F. Cheit, reprinted from AGB REPORTS, vol. 13, no. 6, pp. 4–13, March 1971.*

COLLEGE GENERATIONS—FROM THE 1930S TO THE 1960S, by Seymour M. Lipset and Everett C. Ladd, Jr., reprinted from THE PUBLIC INTEREST, no. 25, Summer 1971.

AMERICAN SOCIAL SCIENTISTS AND THE GROWTH OF CAMPUS POLITICAL ACTIVISM IN THE 1960S, by Everett C. Ladd, Jr., and Seymour M. Lipset, reprinted from SOCIAL SCIENCES IN-FORMATION, vol. 10, no. 2, April 1971.

THE POLITICS OF AMERICAN POLITICAL SCIENTISTS, by Everett C. Ladd, Jr., and Seymour M. Lipset, reprinted from PS, vol. 4, no. 2, Spring 1971.*

THE DIVIDED PROFESSORIATE, by Seymour M. Lipset and Everett C. Ladd, Jr., reprinted from CHANGE, vol. 3, no. 3, pp. 54–60, May 1971.*

JEWISH ACADEMICS IN THE UNITED STATES: THEIR ACHIEVEMENTS, CULTURE AND POLI-TICS, by Seymour M. Lipset and Everett C. Ladd, Jr., reprinted from AMERICAN JEWISH YEAR BOOK, 1971.

THE UNHOLY ALLIANCE AGAINST THE CAMPUS, by Kenneth Keniston and Michael Lerner, reprinted from NEW YORK TIMES MAGAZINE, November 8, 1970.

PRECARIOUS PROFESSORS: NEW PATTERNS OF REPRESENTATION, by Joseph W. Garbarino, reprinted from INDUSTRIAL RELATIONS, vol. 10, no. 1, February 1971.*

. . . AND WHAT PROFESSORS THINK: ABOUT STUDENT PROTEST AND MANNERS, MORALS, POLITICS, AND CHAOS ON THE CAMPUS, by Seymour Martin Lipset and Everett C. Ladd, Jr., reprinted from PSYCHOLOGY TODAY, November 1970.*

DEMAND AND SUPPLY IN U.S. HIGHER EDUCATION: A PROGRESS REPORT, by Roy Radner and Leonard S. Miller, reprinted from AMERICAN ECONOMIC REVIEW, May 1970.*

RESOURCES FOR HIGHER EDUCATION: AN ECONOMIST'S VIEW, by Theodore W. Schultz, reprinted from JOURNAL OF POLITICAL ECONOMY, vol. 76, no. 3, University of Chicago, May/June 1968.*

INDUSTRIAL RELATIONS AND UNIVERSITY RELATIONS, by Clark Kerr, reprinted from PRO-CEEDINGS OF THE 21ST ANNUAL WINTER MEETING OF THE INDUSTRIAL RELATIONS RESEARCH ASSOCIATION, pp. 15–25.*

*The Commission's stock of this reprint has been exhausted.

NEW CHALLENGES TO THE COLLEGE AND UNIVERSITY, by Clark Kerr, reprinted from Kermit Gordon (ed.), AGENDA FOR THE NATION, The Brookings Institution, Washington, D.C., 1968.*

PRESIDENTIAL DISCONTENT, by Clark Kerr, reprinted from David C. Nichols (ed.), PERSPECTIVES ON CAMPUS TENSIONS: PAPERS PREPARED FOR THE SPECIAL COMMITTEE ON CAMPUS TENSIONS, American Council on Education, Washington, D.C., September 1970.*

STUDENT PROTEST—AN INSTITUTIONAL AND NATIONAL PROFILE, by Harold Hodgkinson, reprinted from THE RECORD, vol. 71, no. 4, May 1970.*

WHAT'S BUGGING THE STUDENTS?, by Kenneth Keniston, reprinted from EDUCATIONAL RECORD, American Council on Education, Washington, D.C., Spring 1970.*

THE POLITICS OF ACADEMIA, by Seymour Martin Lipset, reprinted from David C. Nichols (ed.), PERSPECTIVES ON CAMPUS TENSIONS: PAPERS PREPARED FOR THE SPECIAL COMMITTEE ON CAMPUS TENSIONS, American Council on Education, Washington, D.C., September 1970.*

INTERNATIONAL PROGRAMS OF U.S. COLLEGES AND UNIVERSITIES: PRIORITIES FOR THE SEVENTIES, by James A. Perkins, reprinted by permission of the International Council for Educational Development, Occasional Paper no. 1, July 1971.

FACULTY UNIONISM: FROM THEORY TO PRACTICE, by Joseph W. Garbarino, reprinted from INDUSTRIAL RELATIONS, vol. 11, no. 1, pp. 1–17, February 1972.

MORE FOR LESS: HIGHER EDUCATION'S NEW PRIORITY, by Virginia B. Smith, reprinted from UNIVERSAL HIGHER EDUCATION: COSTS AND BENEFITS, American Council on Education, Washington, D.C., 1971.

ACADEMIA AND POLITICS IN AMERICA, by Seymour M. Lipset, reprinted from Thomas I. Nossiter (ed.), IMAGINATION AND PRECISION IN THE SOCIAL SCIENCES, pp. 211–289, Faber and Faber, London, 1972.

POLITICS OF ACADEMIC NATURAL SCIENTISTS AND ENGINEERS, by Everett C. Ladd, Jr., and Seymour M. Lipset, reprinted from SCIENCE, vol. 176, no. 4039, pp. 1091–1100, June 9, 1972.

THE INTELLECTUAL AS CRITIC AND REBEL, WITH SPECIAL REFERENCE TO THE UNITED STATES AND THE SOVIET UNION, by Seymour M. Lipset and Richard B. Dobson, reprinted from DAEDALUS, vol. 101, no. 3, pp. 137–198, Summer 1972.

THE POLITICS OF AMERICAN SOCIOLOGISTS, by Seymour M. Lipset and Everett C. Ladd, Jr., reprinted from THE AMERICAN JOURNAL OF SOCIOLOGY, vol. 78, no. 1, July 1972.

*The Commission's stock of this reprint has been exhausted.

THE DISTRIBUTION OF ACADEMIC TENURE IN AMERICAN HIGHER EDUCATION, *by Martin Trow, reprinted from* THE TENURE DEBATE, *Bardwell Smith (ed.), Jossey-Bass, San Francisco, 1972.*

THE NATURE AND ORIGINS OF THE CARNEGIE COMMISSION ON HIGHER EDUCATION, *by Alan Pifer, based on a speech delivered to the Pennsylvania Association of Colleges and Universities, Oct. 16, 1972, reprinted by permission of the Carnegie Foundation for the Advancement of Teaching.*

COMING OF MIDDLE AGE IN HIGHER EDUCATION, *by Earl F. Cheit, address delivered to American Association of State Colleges and Universities and National Association of State Universities and Land-Grant Colleges, Nov. 13, 1972.*